journeys of faithfulness

stories of life and faith
for young christian women

sarah clarkson

journeys of faithfulness

sarah clarkson

apologia WholeHeart™
FAITH-BUILDING TOOLS FOR THE FAMILY

Journeys of Faithfulness

Published by Apologia/WholeHeart,
an imprint of Apologia Press
a division of Apologia Educational Ministries, Inc.
1106 Meridian Plaza, Suite 340–220
Anderson, Indiana 46016
www.apologia.com

Manufactured in the USA
First Printing: March 2012

ISBN: 978-1-935495-85-7

Cover Design: Alpha Advertising, Sidell, IL
Book Design: Andrea Martin, andreamartindesigns4you.blogspot.com

Printed by Victor Graphics, Inc., Baltimore, MD

Unless otherwise indicated, Scripture quotations are from:
The Holy Bible, New International Version © 1973, 1984
by International Bible Society, used by permission of
Zondervan Publishing House.

Other Scripture quotations are from:
New American Standard Bible® (NASB) © 1960, 1977, 1995
by the Lockman Foundation. Used by permission.

*To Joy, heart of my heart, kindred spirit, and best beloved sister
in all the world. You have shown me what it means to be full to
bursting with the love and life of God. I treasure you.*

contents

part one

Mary & Martha

marched into the fray of vegetables, fruit, and raised voices with relish. Mary walked, as always, a little behind with the basket. The sun rose hot and swift that day, and when they reached the final stall on their rounds, Mary sighed. The War of the Flowers, as she secretly named it, was nigh. Martha insisted that no handful of field lilies ought to cost more than a copper, while the flower woman, Ruth, insisted they were worth at least three. Wits and words were flung to astonishing lengths in this weekly fight, so Mary set the basket down and stretched the stiffness out of her back.

She glanced up the street, where the narrow dirt alley whirred with market-day color. At the farthest end, she glimpsed the cool, blue corner near the synagogue. The air was always damp and strangely sweet down there, and she glanced again with longing eyes.

Martha was deep in the heat of battle now. So Mary backed a step away, then another step and another. She would be back before Martha knew she had gone.

She walked slowly past the booths at first, running her fingers along the cool silks and scratchy weaves in admiration, her eyes hungry and glad for the hues of mounded fruits and bunched flowers. Alone now, she remembered to glance up, her timid eyes catching the eager gaze of the merchants with their quick, broad smiles. One old woman caught her shy smile and pressed a flower into her hand. Mary could not help a small grin as she walked on.

Finally, she reached the shadows. Their hush fell over her flushed face and robed her in their cool as she leaned against the stones of the synagogue. How good to be still, enveloped in calm. Gradually, she heard the buzz on the other side of the stones and her curiosity drove her to creep up near the entrance and set her ear to the shadows inside. She loved to listen to the rabbi discuss the Torah with his disciples, loved the mystery that lingered in the words of the prophets. These were the words of the God who had made her. When she heard these words, she felt that perhaps he saw her, even if no one else did.

But today a clamor inside the synagogue chased away the usual hush. A feverish tone heightened the voices of the young men, while conversations buzzed in countless whispers among the men huddled in small groups outside the synagogue door. Yet through it all came a single voice, low and rich, sometimes calm, sometimes eager. She did not recognize the voice and hovered nearer, hoping to catch few words.

"No, no, you have it wrong," she heard the voice exclaim, "the law is not God. God is love, and he so loved his people that he sent his Son to do what the law cannot, to save you from your sin. The God of Abraham, Isaac, and Jacob is the God of love."

The sharp breath escaped her before she could stop it. The thought of God as love stirred her lonely heart, plumbing the quiet depths of her yearning, and she could not turn away. The group soon broke up for the midday meal, and the young men and rabbis pouring out of the shadows into the light of noon. Mary pulled back and drew her shawl close as they passed. But she would not move or return to her place with Martha and the village women until she had seen the owner of that voice—the voice that said God was love.

She flinched as her brother came out the door and saw her.

Lazarus stared for an instant, his lean, young face confused. Mary knew it wasn't proper for her to lurk around doors, to linger among the men. His eyes shot puzzled, if gentle, irritation at his usually docile sister. As men poured out of the synagogue, he nodded toward the market, where Martha's sturdy figure was plainly visible even from this distance. Mary shook her head and averted her eyes as the last of the crowd came out.

Then, there he was.

She knew him immediately. Only that face, firm yet lined with compassion, only those eyes, brown and friendly, could have owned the gentle voice. She stared, unaware of the others, unable to move. He was talking with a young man whose eyes blazed with argument, but he said a final word, put a hand of peace of the man's shoulder and turned. In that instant he smiled as if he had been expecting to see only her, and his eyes were filled with something that puzzled and gladdened Mary's heart: welcome.

"Ah, Rabbi," Lazarus said, plainly miffed at Mary's boldness and feeling pressed to explain her presence, "this is my sister,"

"Mary."

The teacher spoke her name in harmony with Lazarus, but she heard only the rabbi's voice. For he saw her. He knew her. Not just her name, but all of her. In that moment she knew that he saw everything: the love she hoarded within her and the ache she felt at being forgotten. He saw the deep

Martha would just have to wait. She stepped up to Anna's door.

Martha beat the batter as if it were Mary. She glared into her bowl and smacked it on the wooden table and growled under her breath. Left alone, again. Left to cook and tend, to fetch the water and greet the guests. Left by a sister who was forever happy these days, while Martha herself felt only harried. No one, she thought as she gave the batter a last, devastating stroke, knew the amount of work her life demanded. They all seemed to think food fell hot from the sky. She maintained her household and fed multitudes, and they all, siblings and honored guests alike, pranced about enjoying her the fruits of her labor, and never did anyone think what it cost Martha. No one ever saw.

Mary ducked in the door.

Martha shot her a daggered glance and shoved a bowl into her hands. "What took you so long?"

"I'm sorry, Martha. Anna needed help."

"Old Anna? Oh, I can just see the two of you gossiping the day away. You're always with your head in the clouds while I do all the work down here in the real world. I despair of you, Mary. Now hurry up, chop these onions. The Master and all those men arrived while you were out, and they are upstairs waiting for their dinner."

"He's here?"

Mary's face was like the sun in the morning, and it maddened Martha. She was like a lovelorn girl when Jesus was near. Martha rolled her eyes and did not deign to answer.

"Martha, if we finish quickly, we can go listen to him. You must join us tonight and hear all that he says. He loves it when we come to him."

Martha whirled about, stalked over to where Mary sat with her work, and glared down at her. "Mary, the Master doesn't care that we listen as long as we serve. You act as if he is personally concerned with your presence. He's not. No, no argument. I'm going to fetch water, since you apparently forgot. See if you can get the main dishes on the table without me. That would be a miracle worthy of Jesus himself."

And refusing to see the hurt that kindled in Mary's eyes, Martha marched from the house and into the night. The chill of the air cooled her a bit, and by the time she reached the well, the palpitation of her heart had slowed. She sat on the stones that rimmed the well, aware abruptly of how her bones begged her to sit, how her muscles protested at the thought of heaving the full jar back home. She settled in.

Let Mary shoulder the work for a spell. Let her feel the burden Martha felt every day. *Maybe*, Martha grimaced to herself, *that would force her to be a little more thankful.*

The hush of the wide, starlit sky covered Martha, and in a rare moment of stillness, she looked up. She even marveled. *How beautiful.* She should do this more often. Mary was always gaping at stars and sunsets; perhaps there was something to it after all. What if there was also something to Mary's foolish notion that Jesus noticed, even desired, their presence?

Here, Martha wrinkled her nose. Mary was wrong about that. No rabbi had ever asked her to sit and listen. Only men and the richest of women were offered that grace. Besides, the village was set in its ways. Men listened, women worked. She cooked, Mary dreamed. Her lot was to meet life with head flung high. The Master didn't want her to lounge at his feet and listen; he wanted a hot meal—and that, on time.

It was time to get back. Mary would, of course, be floundering without her. The pull of work straightened Martha and prodded her toward home.

She stepped into the house, all ready for Mary to rush up in a tizzy. But all was silent. The food seemed to be upstairs; Mary had managed that much, at least. All even seemed to be in order, the vegetables covered, and the cooking tools put away. But Mary was gone.

Martha crept a few steps up the stairs and . . . there. She knew it. Mary sat rapt at Jesus' feet, blissfully unaware of Martha or the needs of their guests. Fury rushed like a flood through Martha's soul, filling her mouth, her heart, her eyes. She stomped up the remaining steps.

Mary felt Martha's anger on the back of her head like the heat from an open oven. The silence came first, as tongues stilled and faces turned toward Martha. Even Jesus hushed, and Mary didn't wonder, for the blaze of

Martha's eyes and the hands on her hips demanded attention. Mary cringed.

"Master," Martha barked, her voice hoarse with fury, "do you not care that my sister has left me to do all the work? Then tell her to help me!"

The men raised their eyebrows. Jesus' companion Peter whistled low, and Mary kept her crimson face down as she rose to go.

Then Jesus said, "Martha . . . Martha . . ."

His voice was like a mother wheedling a stubborn child, or the voice of a father who knows the childish fury of the little one he holds and plans to take her anger and hurt away. His voice was a plea, an invitation, a tender command to be still.

> **Martha's noise and bluster hid an aching heart, even as Mary's silence veiled her own.**

"You are worried and distracted about many things. But Martha, there is only one thing needed. Mary has chosen the better part, and it won't be taken away from her."

Martha opened and closed her mouth like a fish out of water, gasping and gaping at the gentle rebuke. Then she fled.

Mary rose then, her face no longer crimson. She glanced at Jesus, caught the slight nod of his head, and followed her sister.

She found Martha crouched on a low stone wall in the alley behind their home. Neither spoke. Mary settled beside Martha and, for a time, they sat quietly in the dark. Then Martha sighed deeply into the night.

"Well, Mary, you were right. He did want you up there. Though I'm pretty sure you are wrong about him wanting me."

Mary saw with sudden clarity that Martha felt lost, as she once had. Martha's noise and bluster hid an aching heart, even as silence had veiled her own. Martha's anger was a cry for someone to see a heart that languished, a soul weary with work. Mary had been found and seen. Now Martha needed to be seen as well.

"Martha, he sent me to find you."

"What?" Mary could feel Martha's skeptical gaze upon her in the dark. "Why? I accused him. I accused the rabbi. Why would he want to be in the same room with me?"

"Because he wants the same joy for you as he has given the others, as he has given me."

"Oh yes, that's right," said Martha wryly, "you chose this 'one good thing.' And what might that be?"

"Just to be with him. To hear all he says, to learn about love. You know, Martha, he really is everything he says. He is the Messiah. And the Messiah is for all people. I think he wants you with him far more than he wants another feast—though he does enjoy those, I've noticed."

Martha laughed, and Mary grinned. She settled closer to Martha on the night-cooled stones, the air dry and starlit around them.

"Martha," said Mary, and put a tentative hand over her sister's, "you have always been the strong one. I know you have had to work hard to care for us. You have always been the queen, always the best of our family."

To her shock, Mary caught the sound of a sob, and from the darkness, Martha spoke, choking on her words.

"No one ever seems to notice. You and Lazarus, always laughing together while I work apart. You with Jesus, like a young girl in love. But I can't be gentle and yielding like you. I'm not quiet. I don't know how to be anything else. No one knows. No one sees. I'm not so strong as you think."

"Oh my Martha, Martha! You must rest," and Mary reached a hand to Martha's. "You must let Jesus love you. I will take care of everything. I'll make all the meals and clean the house. Just come and sit with the Master for a while. I know he's waiting for you."

Mary risked a side glance and saw Martha's lips pursed and her eyes glaring straight ahead.

"They'll laugh at me. All those men. Especially that Peter."

Mary herself laughed then and threw her arms around her stubborn sister.

"If they laugh," she declared with unwonted ferocity, "I'll send the lot of them out the door. And Jesus will help, I'm sure. Come on, Martha. I'm the eldest sister tonight. You're coming with me."

Taking Martha's arm, Mary marched the both of them back into their house. She pulled her lead-footed sister up the stairs until they stood once more in the long, low room where the spice of Martha's feast still scented the air. The men were hunched in small groups, abuzz with discussion, the shadows warm and filled with murmurs. At the far end sat Jesus.

He raised his eyes to Martha's the instant they entered. Lazarus, too, looked up, saw the way Mary tugged Martha along, and instantly moved aside so that a place opened at Jesus' feet. Peter and one or two of the other disciples looked Martha's way with arched eyebrows, but Mary glared at them with such furor that they cowed and dropped their gaze. Then Mary knelt on the ground as Martha stood like a small, troubled girl, her hands in a twist of pleading. She lifted her face to Jesus.

He grinned.

"Martha." His eyes saw her very soul. "I've been waiting for you to come."

devotional

My mother can read me like a book. I remembered this keenly not long ago when I received news of a great score on a college test. I tromped down the stairs into the kitchen to make a celebratory cup of tea. My mom stood over the stove, and I didn't even look her way before she turned and was at my side, eyes arched in curiosity.

"What happened?" she asked.

I spluttered my news, shocked at her quick perception.

But I shouldn't have been surprised. There's not much I can hide from my mother. She can read my heart in just the glance I give her when I walk in the door. When pain is hidden or joy lurks just below the surface, she sees it all. Words only clarify what she already knows from a lifetime of watchful love. She has pondered and known me. I have been the study of her heart since I was born. She knows my soul as few ever will.

Her love is a lot like God's.

Imagine that the Holy One of the universe, Maker of heaven and earth, Savior of mankind, knows us with the tender intimacy of a mother. He knows the small things we love and the great things we hope. He sees our triumphs, our fears. Every atom of your self and soul is held in a gentle understanding beyond what you can fathom.

When I sat down to write the first chapter of this book, I wondered how best to begin. What is the first thing to say about how to walk with God? The natural urge is to start by listing all the things we must do as His followers. Believe this thing and have this sort of faith. Be this kind of person, read this sort of book, and do these kinds of good work. My impulse was to make a list you could check off and call yourself holy. But this, I realized, is the way of Martha.

Martha thought she could make God like her better by serving good food and doing good deeds. Many of us approach God in this way. We start from our own ability, thinking that we must prove our devotion by the amount of service we perform. Busy and determined, we hustle and bustle through life doing all the right things and feeling very irritated by it all. And when we stand before God's throne, we enter with a clamor, noisy in our desperation for Him to notice us, to accept and love us for all we do for Him.

The good part, the great gift that Mary chose, was to leave the clamor behind and simply dwell in the love of God. She sat at the feet of the One who made her and let Him hold the deepest parts of her soul. Mary began a life of holiness by dwelling in the great tenderness of her God. And this is where you and I must begin as well.

Holy living doesn't start with us. We cannot build the house of our lives on a foundation of our own righteous works and the meager obedience we offer. We cannot earn God's love because we obey. God's grace is the first cause. He is the glad-hearted lover who woos us to follow Him with all our hearts. He loves us incredibly, deeply, eternally, and that is why we love Him back and devote our lives to Him.

When you make God's love the foundation of your life, it forms two things that are crucial to a lifelong walk toward what is holy and good. First, you will gain confidence, even boldness in your pursuit of Jesus. The very depth of His love will create a determination in your heart that will bring you to His feet day after day, just like Mary.

Study the customs of Jewish life in Jesus' time and you will find that it was a startling thing for a woman to sit at the feet of a rabbi. This was a place reserved for men, for students of the Torah. Yet Mary had the audacity to walk right in and sit at the feet of her Master, because she recognized the love that waited for her there.

I find it fascinating how Martha, usually the bolder and louder of the sisters, was scandalized by Mary's actions, shocked by the way that love made Mary so bold. When Martha protested Mary's absence in the kitchen, I think that in many ways, she just wanted Jesus to restore the status quo where she could earn points for the work she did and the rules she followed. This unbridled love that upended social expectations, that demanded the whole of her being, scared her.

Jesus refused. He refused to know Martha according to the good deeds she did for Him. Instead, he praised her sister who made the daring choice to seek the great love of the Master and sit at his feet. He upended the expectations of every man and woman in that room by affirming Mary's choice to be a student, to prize the love of God over any other work or concern. Notice that He didn't denigrate work or dishonor Martha for the good work she did. His concern was to make Martha understand where she truly belonged. The rightful place of any heart in this world is to sit in rapt adoration at the feet of God.

Mary was confident of the love of her Lord. Martha was not. Martha was restless with the need to be noticed, noisy with her own fear of being forgotten. Mary walked right into the sacred circle of Jesus' presence and sat down. She knew herself to be known, and it made her bold with love in her soul. When you grasp the love that God has for you, you, too, will seek him out with a confidence beyond what any keeping of rules can inspire.

As we begin this study, as we set out with souls hungry

to know and serve God, let us begin by dwelling in love. Let us sit at the feet of the One whose heart holds all beauty, whose love created every kindness in this world. This is where we must start. This is where we fill ourselves with grace for the journey we have just begun. We start not by walking, but by basking in the great love of Jesus.

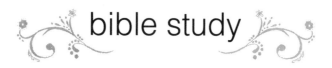 bible study

1 John 4:7–10

What does this passage say about the love of God? Who loved first, God or us? Can you know God apart from His love?

Ephesians 3:14–19

What does it mean to be "rooted and established" in love? Why do you think this is necessary to become "filled with all the fullness of God"?

1 Corinthians 13

You probably have this passage halfway memorized as the standard Christian "behavioral guide." But read it again with fresh eyes and consider that each aspect of love described is exactly what God offers you.

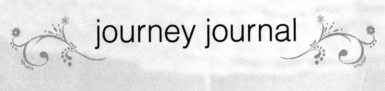

journey journal

chapter two

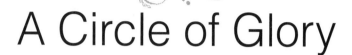

A Circle of Glory

The silence after parting from a beloved is a live, insistent presence. The way the empty air echoes with the laughter of someone who has gone. The way you are left not just with yourself, but the staring absence of someone else. Mary hated the silence that pooled about her. Lazarus, gentle and bright, the brother whose voice was music that filled the hearts of his sisters, was dead.

Mary now understood why people wept and wailed in the presence of death. To her quiet self, weeping had always seemed overly dramatic. But now she knew. Only tears could stave off this void of a never-to-be-relieved silence. Alone now in her tiny room, she sobbed. A river of grief flooded her heart and throat and eyes, keeping the silence at bay and bringing the first comfort she'd known since Lazarus died of a sudden fever four days earlier.

"Stop it."

As if Mary's sobs had summoned her, Martha appeared in the doorway, black-swathed and stolid, head high. Mary groaned. Her first minutes alone in days were now lost. Mourners crammed their little house—clucking, comforting neighbors whose affectionate ministrations were not to be denied. Mary had thought herself safe. She too would die, she wanted to shout at Martha, if she could not have five minutes to herself. But the words never escaped her lips. No sound came at all, for how could she speak in the tortured presence of Martha?

"Mary, we must not cry. Please."

Mary ceased crying even before Martha came to her and, kneeling, rubbed away the tears in strokes that left red paths down Mary's skin. Martha's eyes gleamed black, staring like dark gems in the desert of her face where the skin stretched thin, etched deep by the cold of weariness and the heat of grief. Her cheeks hollowed, as if by hunger, Martha stared ahead, and Mary glimpsed the unspoken pain that devoured the life in her even as they stood together.

"We must be strong," Martha spoke low again, her voice thick. "We are two lone women now. We cannot fall apart, even now. We must keep our heads and bear this. You must do it with me. Because we are, truly, alone."

Mary now took Martha's face in her hands, not flinching at the fever heat of her sister's skin, nor the hard aversion of the dark eyes. "We're not alone," she whispered to her steeled sister, coaxing forth the tears, the yielding that would heal her of the hard grief. "Our friends will help us,"

"What friends?" Martha whispered, flinching in disgust. "What can those gossiping magpies and their long-faced husbands do for us now? Everyone we needed has been taken from us. Father and Mother first, then Jacob—oh Jacob, my husband. And now even Lazarus. He wasn't much use, but he was a man of the house. And he was gentle. Such a sweet boy . . ." Martha's voice cracked.

"Shush, Martha, shush. We are not alone. Jesus—"

Martha shoved herself out of Mary's grasp, and her face went crimson.

"Jesus?" she hissed, "Jesus? He's not here, Mary. Did you notice? He didn't come. We begged for him to come, to save his friend. And he. Did. Not. Come." Martha stepped back, bent double, her arms wrapped round herself as if she were in deathly pain. "Do not say his name to me. Master, we called him. Rabbi. Healer. What of these has he been to us? He neither came nor healed. He abandoned us, and he is no longer my master."

She spat the words, and Mary bore their spite, knowing that Martha yearned to strike Jesus and instead could only hurt the one who loved him. Words rose like flames in Martha's eyes, Mary saw, but at that moment three wide-eyed women tumbled into the room.

"Mary, Martha," they clucked, ruffled and restless as hens, "the Master is here. Jesus is here! He's coming down the main road and making straight for your house."

Martha turned, eyes ablaze with fury. White and wordless, she shoved through the group and strode out the door. Chirping with surprise, the women pattered after her. And Mary, arms wrapped round herself, chin hunched into her dark cloak, was finally left to her peace.

Martha could not walk fast enough. She stumbled and then picked up her skirts and her feet and ran. Oh, how she hated him! After this she never wanted to see that false face, that cunning kindness again. He had tricked her and abandoned her. Martha felt that if she could not reach Jesus just now, stand before him with the hard, hot weight of her grief like a coal in her hands to fling in his face, she would die.

Her fury was such that the rumor of it ran before her, and the men around Jesus fell back a step. But he did not. He strode forward steadily, so that Martha met him sooner than she thought and skidded to a halt, panting. But she was at no loss. Tall and grim, in the dark, rough-woven cloak of her mourning, she drew herself up to the Master with the eyes of a tiger stalking its prey.

"Master," she spat in greeting and bobbed her head so that she mocked him with the unbroken glare of her eyes. Every muscle straining, she moved closer, not waiting for him to speak. "If you had been here, my brother would not have died."

> **His goodness was real as the ground on which she stood.**

Martha stopped, choking on her accusation. This was not what she had meant to say. She wanted to scream that he was a liar, a trickster, a wandering poser who ate people's food and won their hearts and spoke words of hope, then disappeared when pain showed its ugly face. He was no better than a street magician pulling feathers from people's ears while his servants picked people's pockets. This was what she meant to scream right in his face, in front of those he loved.

Yet she could not.

Her own heart betrayed her and spoke the truth she could not bear to behold.

He could have saved Lazarus, could have healed her brother. Jesus chose not to, and this was the deep, garish hurt. She knew that he was no charlatan, no cheap conjurer. The words he had spoken all those evenings in her home, the kindness he gave her, the life he brought to her family were true as the sun that warmed the earth. If he was false, then life itself and the air she breathed must be false, because his goodness was real as the ground on which she stood. She remembered this anew as she watched him bear her words, and she saw once more the gentleness unflinching, the mercy steady in his eyes. His gaze upon her was a summons. She almost yielded, almost lurched into the arms she knew would open to catch her.

But she held back, confused. Jesus was the Son of God who spoke life to all creation, so how could he allow death? How could he let his beloved suffer? She fell abruptly to her knees, blind and frail in her confusion. She could no longer meet his eyes.

Oh, how she had prayed in the dark of those final days as Lazarus lay sweating his life away! A frightened, childlike prayer offered in her darkest hour, her faith fragile as a spider's web. Until the last she had hoped, yet no answer had come.

So now she would beg. If the Master wanted dramatic obeisance, she would give it. Yahweh must be closer to the pagan gods than she thought, reluctant to answer until his followers wrung every drop of tortured self onto the altar.

"Please" she said. "Even now, I know that God will give you whatever you ask."

She groveled in the dust. Pebbles dented her hands. Fine, brown dirt and the detritus of the earth filled her sight, and she would not, could not, lift her eyes higher. She felt, more than saw, the feet of a gathering crowd staring down at her. Martha, the self-assured and strong, was finally humbled. None would join her, she knew, in this brown kneeling valley of loss. None would plead or wait with her. None would stoop to grieve beside her.

None but one.

"Martha."

Her eyes flicked up, and she was astonished. Jesus was there. The Son of God knelt next to her in the dirt in front of all these witnesses. Jesus sat with her in the echoing valley of her barren, stripped-down soul. She leaned forward, her lips open with shock.

"Martha," he said again, demanding all her attention now. "Your brother will rise again."

Again, she almost believed him, almost stumbled childlike into the surety that his love inspired. Then she realized his meaning, and she closed her eyes and shut him out.

"Yes, Lord, I know. In the resurrection. At the last day."

Small comfort that gave. She wanted life now. Hope now. Death had defined her for so long. First, a plague had taken her mother and father, the daylight of her world. Then a field accident had taken Jacob, the burly, blustering, merry-hearted husband who took her in and made a home of laughter for her and her siblings. With him, Martha had almost believed in joy again. But after she buried Jacob, Martha did not leave the house for a month.

When she finally emerged, she was hard and bright. She ruled with the tenacity of death itself. No longer would she cry like Mary. The luxury of a tender heart had passed her by. She died to joy so that she could protect the ones she loved. She sheltered frail Lazarus and bossed gentle Mary, and she made a household that would stand as a small fortress against poverty or illness. Yet once again death tricked her and stole the very thing she had given her soul to protect.

Through it all, through every death, God but watched. Never had he saved or stayed the iron fist of loss as it crushed her. And now God stared out at her through the gentle eyes of the man who called himself Son to the Almighty. And this God demanded that she believe in life. "Lazarus will live again," he said, asking her to believe that he had not betrayed her.

"I am the resurrection. I am the life." He spoke now with a vehemence that drew her from her introspection. He grabbed both her hands and caught her eyes. Life knelt before her, kind and fierce, his eyes a fire warming her face. "Anyone who believes in me will live, even if his body dies. And Martha, everyone who believes in me, who lives in me, will never die. Never. Do you believe this?"

His question was spoken so quietly, the crowd did not hear. But Martha did, and she knew that her answer would define her life. The pain of her doubt creased her face, and she rocked, aching, trying to form an answer. Lazarus was dead, her husband was dead, and grief was a pit in her soul. How could she believe the promise of Jesus?

But how could she not? Stripped now of every prop that ever staid her faith, bereft of her brother, kneeling in the dirt, Martha looked back at Jesus. And she knew. Either life beyond the hands of death and hope beyond all the grief of the world were true, or they were not. She could not dabble in doubt and think it would not kill her. Faith was not a toy she could pick up when she liked, then set it down. She must fling herself body and soul into the choice.

Could she choose doubt? Choose to believe that death was the end of all things, that love would be crushed, that hope was a fancy for children? No.

Only one choice remained. She must trust in a power beyond her sight, beyond her comprehension. She must fling a cry of faith into the very face of death, stare it down, and declare it somehow beaten, because this was the only answer. If all that Jesus said and did was true, then life must be working to turn back death even now.

> **Only one choice remained: She must trust in a power beyond her comprehension.**

Her choice was made, and she opened her hands, yielding her spirit to the Master as a strong, strangled cry broke from her throat.

"Yes, yes, I believe!"

The crowd stirred around her, and Martha scrambled suddenly to her feet, eyes brilliant with the words that burgeoned suddenly to life in her, like the gathering of light at dawn. Her old self settled back on her shoulders, and she stood straight, placed her hands on her hips, took a deep breath, and spoke what she must. "Yes," she declared, her voice strong and golden. "I believe. You are the Christ, the Son of the living God. Yes, I believe."

And then she began weeping as grief and faith rushed together within her and made a flood of joy unlike anything she had ever felt. Jesus opened his arms, and she fell into them. This was her truth. From this moment forth she would walk in the love of her gentle God. Though death strike her heart, she would be safe in the firm hands of this One whose robe was dusty from kneeling with her, whose hands were striped by her tears. She was sure now of a love beyond any sorrow and better than any joy. Yes, she believed.

"Mary, Mary! Where are you?"

The vibrancy of the voice startled Mary from her thoughts. The cry was Martha's, she knew, yet she questioned her senses. Martha's voice was changed, as though some weight had been lifted, some shadow removed. Mary knew with a thrill that this was the voice of Martha's girlhood, the voice that sang music from stone to rafter in their younger days, before the world was broken.

"I'm here, Martha. Here," she called.

Suddenly a warm, black-swathed hurricane threw itself around her. Martha was hugging her. This took Mary a few seconds to digest, and with shaking hands she returned the embrace.

Martha was wet, drenched in tears. They slicked her face and soaked her scarf. As Mary pulled gently back, she saw in Martha's eyes a light springing up like water from some deep well. The anguished lines in Martha's face were filled in with love, the hard, red anger washed away.

Mary began to weep at the sight, and this time Martha did not stop her. They clung together, faces hidden in each other in grief and joy. Finally Martha whispered, "The Master wants to see you."

Mary rushed from the house. A bevy of women followed, but she didn't notice them. Swift in her love as Martha had been in her anger, Mary ran up the road to meet Jesus. No hesitation stayed her feet. No anger restrained her. She fled swiftly to the heart that had already cradled her soul for the past four days. Straight to the arms that would shelter her through every darkness.

Mary knelt at Jesus' feet, and he knelt to meet her, to hold her as she shook with grief. The villagers encircled them just as they had gathered around Martha and Jesus, their curiosity now replaced by a gentle longing.

Mary lifted her face to Jesus, and hope glimmered in her eyes like the first hint of dawn. "If you had been here," she said, "my brother would not have died." Yet this was not an accusation. She trusted the Master, trusted his love. She saw that Martha had been healed—Martha whose soul had been as lifeless as Lazarus's body. Life was already turning death backwards, so she would cling to the source of life—and wait.

There was a light in Jesus' eyes as he watched her face. "Take me to the tomb," he said.

At once, there was a mass of feet moving and elbows nudging as the crowd pressed close to Jesus. "This way, Rabbi," said wizened men and squirming children alike, careless of anything but his favor.

They reached the place, just beyond the edge of the village, a cave fashioned into a handsome tomb. The crowd stopped well outside the entrance of the tomb. This was a place of death, and no one wanted to draw too near. So Jesus stepped to the tomb alone. He placed his hand on the stone that sealed his friend away from those who loved him. He bent his head and wept.

Martha watched and marveled that the Son of God should stand at the site of her loss and share her grief. Mary watched and ached to see love stand at the place of broken hearts and bear her sorrow.

The crowd watched with faces softened, eyes, even the old ones, misty with tears. Here was a rabbi who did not stand apart from their grief, spouting platitudes while widows and children wept. This was a teacher who would grieve alongside them, who would honor their pain and make it his own. A few crusty ones—crusty not in face or bones, but in their souls—stood apart and whispered that a healer of blind men ought to have saved his friend. But these were unceremoniously jabbed in the ribs and shushed by their neighbors. After all, you could not doubt a rabbi who was willing to weep.

The whole crowd leaned forward as if to comfort him. Suddenly, Jesus straightened, struck the tombstone with his fist, and turned.

> **This was a teacher who would grieve alongside them.**

"Take away this stone," he said.

His command was met with silence. Eyes wide and whitened as sea stones stared at him all around.

Then Jesus smiled. He called to his disciples, "Come, quickly, help me. Move the stone." His words gathered vim and volume, and brightness glimmered in his eyes as five men heaved and hacked at the stone.

"Lord," said Martha, squirming, her hands twisting, her face blotchily flushed. "He's been dead for four days. He'll stink."

Mary swore afterwards, that Jesus rolled his eyes and laughed, but Martha never saw it—she was too busy cringing and wishing she could keep her practical observations to herself.

"Martha." Jesus was grinning. "Did I not tell you that if you believed, you would see the glory of God?"

The stone was rolled away. A black, dusty hole gaped in the mountain wall, and dust motes fled from it into the grey light. Jesus turned to the shadow and planted himself dead center, face uplifted. "Father," he cried so that everyone could hear, "I thank you that you have always heard me. I know you always do, but I say this aloud today for these people here, so that they may know you have sent me."

The words struck at the darkness and stone like a hammer, ringing from rock to rock, hard and brilliant, chipping away at death and fear.

"Lazarus! Come forth!"

In a symphony of echoes, the command rose up and shook the air. In an instant, the crowd heard a scrabbling inside the tomb, the pat and swish of feet in the rocky dust, the plink of stones kicked out from moving feet. Jesus' cry still echoed round as a slight, linen-swathed figure stumbled into the cave's dark entrance.

The crowd stood like dead men, watching. Not a muscle twitched among them. Breaths were barely drawn as Jesus stepped up and unwound the slender, white strips of cloth from the figure's face. First came eyes like the brown earth washed in sunlight and newly turned in spring. They glittered with life. Then, inch by inch, the face, firm with joy, until the lips were free and Lazarus met the eyes of his Lord.

"Master," he said, tears in his laughing eyes, an imp's grin on his boyish mouth, "you called?"

And the silence of the tomb was shattered in a cacophony of laughter. Wild echoes of joy leapt and cried as the crowd roared to life. People danced and laughed, grabbed each other by the arm and spun each other round. Mary tumbled forward and grabbed her brother. Martha could not decide whether to sob or laugh and so choked herself merrily on both as she clutched at Lazarus' free arm and met the life in his eyes.

"Martha," he blurted, "you've been crying. You'd think someone had died."

And then she laughed indeed, bent double with a joy that broke and healed her all at once. She laughed as the circle of death was filled with dancing because love had come among them and had not failed. She laughed as her eyes were filled with the sight of the glory of God.

devotional

I was in the house alone just as a winter's dusk poured darkness through all the windows. A conference weekend loomed, and I was packing in my room. Actually, I was whirling about to very loud music, attempting to turn the exercise of stuffing my suitcase into an aerobic dance. I put my foot down for a vigorous pirouette to the blood-quickening *uilleann* pipes of a Thomas Newman song. To my shock, my leg buckled and my knee gave an astounding pop. Next thing I knew, I was on the floor, back against the wall, legs at odd angles, my right ankle twitching. I rubbed my knee, trying to calm my ankle. I rocked back and forth as feeling came back and pain rushed in.

And then I cried. The shock of it brought tears. The pain was low grade, but I was scared at what I might have done. As I sat there watching my toes twitch, I wept big, babyish tears. I asked myself if I were two years old, and my brain calmly answered no. I asked myself if I intended to let a little knee pain cow me from daring rescues, hikes across the English moors, or relief work in a war-torn country (all of which I plan to do). Of course not. I hobbled my way to a chair and took deep, decisive breaths. But each strong suck of air came out shredded by a sob. I couldn't stop.

I soon realized that I was crying not just for my knee, but for months and years of pain. As if some prison door had been shoved open, I was suddenly assailed by every grief and struggle I had locked away in my heart over the past months. My year had been one of great loneliness. My search for community at church, for like-hearted friends, had left me mostly empty handed. My health was failing again, and the doctors had no idea why. Family issues and private hurts tore at my heart, while the sense of God's absence only grew. But I had determinedly locked the pain away, bent on courage and the will to keep on.

Now, for some odd reason, my bruised little knee was the last straw. The extra hurt that broke my strength. I couldn't understand why God would not intervene in my problems and change my life. I could not feel Him with me. Sitting in my room that winter's night, I felt the hot, barren dark of despair. I yearned to yell at my Maker, "Where were you? You could have saved me and you didn't!"

Where is God when we suffer? It's an age-old question that rattles in the heart of anyone who decides to follow God. Suffering will come and when it does, it will shake your faith like nothing else. I remember my naive shock when pain first really found me. The world seemed abruptly black, and God went from a sure goodness to a distant deity beyond my comprehension. *Lord*, I protested, *I thought you were supposed to be nice.*

The great destructiveness of pain is that it causes us to question the very love of God. I have asked so many times in my life, *Why would God allow me to suffer when I have given everything to him?* One "Job's friend" of mine suggested that it was because God wanted me to be holy. But I found it hard to believe that God looked down from on high at twelve-year-old me, scratched His divine chin, and decreed a personal regimen of pain to develop righteousness.

Zap! *An emotional crisis at sixteen. That ought to keep her humble.* Zap! *Deep loneliness. Now she'll have to depend on me.* Zap! *A strange illness that no doctor can quite identify or treat. Nothing like frailty to let her know she's weak.* Zap! *Five moves, two cross-country. Best not to let her get attached to anyone.* Zap! *A popped knee and loneliness and exhaustion.*

The mere thought is enough to send me screaming incoherently in the opposite direction, away from my God and Savior.

It sent Martha screaming straight to Jesus, tears on her face and accusation on her lips. She didn't even ask why, she stated the agonizing obvious: God could have saved, and He didn't. She thought that made Jesus the cruelest person she knew. I believe her statement that day was a charge she wanted Him to answer in front of the whole village, in front of the world.

But Jesus answered this wild-eyed, weeping woman with a question about her faith. His question was not a request for information; it was a challenge. "I am the life. Do you believe this?" With this question, He forced Martha to go back to the core of her faith. Did she really believe that God loved her? Did she believe His words were true? This is the question asked of all of us when we suffer. In pain, we are pushed toward the deepest belief we will ever hold. We all become Martha, and Jesus' question is directed at us. When I sat on my floor that night, sobbing, I knew that I, too, had to answer that fundamental question.

First, I ask myself if I believe in the person of Jesus. I cannot look upon Him without a softening of my heart. In Christ, I find a God who suffers. Jesus is not an impassive deity who zaps us with grief and watches our pain. He is fully human and fully God, the One who takes on our flesh and weeps along with us. This God so passionately loved us that He stepped down from His throne into the dirt and grief to heal us. He sweat blood the night he was killed (Luke 22:44). He wept when his friend died (John 11:35). He looked on the crowds at Jerusalem and felt compassion for all the lost, tear-stricken souls (Luke 19:41–42). This is where I begin to deal with my pain, with a

Lord who has not only known my grief but bears it with me.

But once I have grasped that fact, God pushes me even deeper into his grace. He asks a second question of me just as He did Martha: *I am the resurrection and the life. Do you believe this, Sarah?*

And that is where the harder part comes. This is where I must choose faith when the reality of pain is still before me. This is where I enter the wild territory called redemption. From the first day of creation, God has been characterized by His will to take what is dark and fill it with light. This didn't change when sin entered the world. God is still the Creator. He still calls forth beauty from ashes, from formless grief (Isaiah 61:3). The great faith that Jesus asks of us in our suffering is to believe that He can restore life to what is dead. This is what Aslan, in *The Lion, the Witch and the Wardrobe*, calls "the Deep Magic . . . working backwards."

We humans cannot imagine that anything good could come of suffering. But one of the deepest, most life-changing truths I have ever found is that God can and will take my loneliness, doubt, rejection, hurt, and yearning and turn them into something beautiful in my life.

I see this in the way compassion has grown in my heart. Loneliness has opened my eyes to other hurting people, to the girl lurking at the edge of a group, to the kid about to leave church because he feels rejected.

I see it in the way sickness has humbled me, helping me to understand how little control I have over the world and myself. That sounds like a bad thing, yet it has caused me to run to God, to trust His goodness in a way nothing else ever has.

I see it in my love for beauty. I have learned that the best way to keep my heart alive in the midst of struggle is to light a candle, listen to music, read a great story, or make a great meal. This habit of turning a dark moment into one of creation has helped me to write stories, to compose music, to craft my room and life to be rich with lovely things.

To live a life of redemption means to trust God even with the pain you cannot understand. To reject the way of redemption leads only to a life of bitterness. If you cannot trust God with your pain, then you will hate Him for it. I think that's what Martha saw in that awful moment of truth. If she chose to reject Jesus, then the only option left was death. Her only remaining truth would be the reality of her suffering and the power it had to take away all she loved and leave her in bitterness of heart.

I'll admit, redemption can be slow. Redemption isn't always easy or apparent because it is God's grace working amidst utter brokenness. But if you choose to embrace this way of walking through pain, you will see the very life of God become real in your circumstances. You will find the ability to hope where you never expected it. And you will see God strengthen your heart and guide you through the darkness.

That night in my chair, I chose to believe in Jesus once again. I gave Him my weariness and pain and trusted Him to turn it into good. With Martha, I said, "Yes, I believe." And I know I will see the glory of God's love as it redeems all my darkness into light.

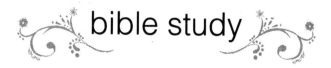

bible study

Ephesians 1:15-20

What is the hope of Christ's calling? What would you say are the riches of His power in your own life as a believer? How does the resurrection of Jesus bring hope and power to your daily life?

Jeremiah 3:19-25

Why does the prophet have hope? Can you list "new mercies" in your life today?

Psalm 139:12

What darkness do you face in your own life? Do you believe that God is stymied by your struggle? Read all of Psalm 139 and list every way God knows and cares for the intimate details of your life.

Colossians 1

Read this whole passage and think of what it means in light of your current struggle or pain. This is your story. How does it change the way you look at life here in the broken place?

journey journal

47

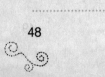

chapter three

The Hush of Love

Martha's gift was to be brilliant, to shimmer in the light of people's eyes as a polished shell glimmers in sunlight. Martha's gift was to be happy, to gather joy easily, spin energy from the daily threads of talk and cooking, love and serving. This gift Mary had long envied, for it seemed to her that in Martha's world the whirl of gladness left no space or stillness for the voices that whispered always to Mary in her silence.

Of late, with her happiness new and tender as a baby's, Martha had been giddy as a girl. The miracle of Lazarus's life and the miracle of faith had cleansed the hardened woman from her soul. Martha laughed now. She touched and loved. The innocent joy of it brought strange, sudden tears to Mary's eyes. What a man, what a Lord, their Jesus, to turn the hard brilliance of Martha's pain into this yielding girlhood!

Now, for the first time in her life, Mary yearned to *be* Martha. This want was doubled by a sensation Mary had never known before, that of being older, cannier than her sister. For Mary could not catch her sister's elusive giddiness no matter how determinedly she chased it. Her joy in her Lord had not changed her quiet nature, the slowness of her tongue, nor the sharpness of her eyes. And it was what she saw now in her quiet that shut her out in a cold air of fear and made her wise as she never had wished to be.

His eyes. Those eyes that had seen her as no other had. How could Mary now fail to see them in turn? To see, she supposed, was her gift. Not to attract eyes, but to witness their secrets. And in Jesus' eyes, pain pooled and gathered until a tide of sorrow nearly filled his face. To Mary, this shadow was the scream of wind before a storm that portended merciless destruction, for it held the darkness of death. Mary had seen it before, seen the blackness of dying swallow the light in Lazarus's brown eyes the night of his death. Now death stared out at her from the face of the man whom she believed to be life itself.

The wonder was that no one else saw. No one else wanted to, she thought. For months now, Jesus had spoken to them of how the Son of Man must suffer to save His people. He told them that he would indeed die, soon, and he spoke it in words Mary could not deny. He spoke of the snake of Moses lifted in the wilderness. He spoke of taking up a cross. But His followers wanted a living, conquering Messiah. The miracles of Jesus—blind men healed, lepers cleansed, and Lazarus raised from the dead—shot through the sky of Israel like a star of mighty omen. The Messiah had come, and surely God's people were to be delivered once and for all.

But did all these followers of Jesus think that darkness and bondage would shrink back like a cowed dog because they desired it? Surely they knew that freedom came at a price. That Jesus would willingly give his life, Mary knew. And that his heart broke with grief, she saw and nearly writhed in beholding.

Tonight she watched him as she served with Martha. Tonight his shoulders curved with weariness, and his eyes were ringed by exhaustion. In and out of the close, small room she went, dodging the lounging men, casting a smile at Lazarus, stopping to share some word of news with one of Jesus' disciples. The meal was especially good—lightness of heart made Martha lighter of hand in the kitchen, and her cooking had only improved. Laughter spilled from several corners, and it seemed a pleasant evening with the Master. Yet every time she glanced at Jesus, Mary could only see the storm in his eyes. By the time she had plunked the last dish on the table, she felt as if two hands were crushing her heart, and she hurried downstairs to her room.

She crouched in the corner where her pallet lay and put her face in her hands. The dark and quiet eased her. She could think now, slower, clearer. *Do something, you must do something*, her heart cried over and over again. She yearned to think of some gift, some comfort to ease Jesus in his lonely pain. Her eyes fell upon the small wooden box that sat in a corner of her room. Mary took it in her hands and ran her finger along the intricate stars carved on its top. She opened the little box, set it on the ground, and began removing its treasures one by one.

These were the small, precious things of her life, the few possessions she claimed in all the earth. Little things mostly, of value to her heart alone. The tiny camel carved for her by Lazarus when he was a boy in apology for a prank. The dark, worn shawl that had belonged to her dead mother, still fragrant with her scent after all these years. A small hair comb with a tiny pearl at its tip that Mary had worn at Martha's wedding.

Mary removed the alabaster bottle last and cradled it in her hands. This was a treasure indeed, a jewel of the heart, but also a prize for which any merchant would pay a handsome price. Pure nard it was, sweetest scent of the Orient. Mary traced the delicate vines etched in the alabaster, caressed the wax that sealed the precious liquid in until the grand day of its breaking. This had been a gift from her father. The year before fever struck him down,

> **She would anoint him, honor him, to strengthen his heart for the hurt he must bear.**

he had called his girls to him and given them both a single alabaster vial. For the future, he said. For dowries or houses or whatever their hearts might someday desire.

The gift had become Mary's greatest treasure. In it, she clung to the love she had lost—and the love she hoped to find. She sometimes thought, and blushed, that it was like herself, the little jar. Unornamented on the outside, plain, waiting for a buyer who knew the price of its precious contents.

Now she gazed at the one real treasure she owned, this secret symbol of love given, the sign of her hope for love to come again. To give this to any man was a gift of sheer extravagance. The love of a lifetime must be the cause of its giving. Now was the time. A love large as her life, a love to claim and hold her throughout her days had indeed found her, and this would be the seal she would set upon it.

There was so little she could do for her Lord. She could not defend Jesus against mobs. She could not hold back the coming storm. She could not make men see the truth he proclaimed. Nard was the perfume of love, but it was also the oil of anointing for the dead. She was not sure what pain awaited the Master, so she would anoint him, honor him, to strengthen his heart for the hurt he must bear. Love and death in a fragrance together, her heart and her treasure broken for him. This would be her gift.

She put away the other things. The vial she wrapped in a shawl and held it close to her. She stood, resting for a last instant in the hush of her solitude. A slender cord of twilight fell through the window and traced a silver line on the floor. The quiet of night grew rich and stilled her heart. With a last breath, she left the room and ran up the stairs.

The voices were louder now. The minute she entered, she saw that an argument had broken out. Several disciples stood with reddened faces. Lazarus sat upright, seeking to quiet those around him. Martha sat silent in a corner, her eyes darting from this speaker to that as the voices leapt high and angry across the tables.

"No!" stormed Peter, "No, Master, surely you don't mean it. The Messiah must lead his people to victory."

"How could we continue if you were gone, Master?" said Philip, his voice low.

"Peter," thundered John, "you are missing it again. The Messiah didn't come to save us from Rome. Do you ever listen?"

Peter leapt to his feet as Simon the Zealot spoke in his defense. "No, Peter's right. What is the Messiah for but to make Israel strong, a ruler of the earth?"

The voices pelted Mary like hard rain. Anger rose in a high wind, and through the maelstrom Mary saw Jesus. His head was bowed and his hands raised as if to bring the men about him to peace, but none of them were watching. None saw him but Mary.

Swift and sure, she crossed the room and knelt in her place at Jesus' feet. The strike of her bottle on the floor crashed through the clamor of voices. The fragrance of nard was a sudden warmth that seeped into the air, the sweet, heady scent of it hushing each tongue. All eyes watched Mary now, but she did not see them.

She saw only the Master, and his eyes were fixed on hers. Over his head and feet she poured the perfume, the amber oil running like melted gold between her fingers as she rubbed and spread the stuff over the tired feet of her Master. *This is my love*, her heart whispered, *the small gift I fling in the face of death.* And when she was done, she knelt, quiet, and closed her eyes.

"Why was this perfume not sold?" The voice shoved the sweetness aside, marring, it seemed to Mary, the peace in which she wished Jesus to rest, and her heart ached that it should be broken.

"Three hundred denarii it would have brought, a fortune to feed the poor," the voice kept on, ridicule roughening its tone. Mary knew this to be Judas, knew the contempt that snarled his lips, knew the shrewd way he watched her.

"Leave her alone!" The command was a blow, and it struck Judas silent.

Mary looked up to see Jesus, face alight with a taut, pure anger that shielded Mary and challenged her accuser. Then his face eased.

"She has done a beautiful thing to me. She has done this to prepare me for my burial." He turned to the others. "You will always have the poor." The sternness of his glare made Judas drop his gaze. "But, my friends, you will not always have me."

He looked down at Mary, his eyes so gentle, so thankful, that Mary put her hands to her heart for the pain of her love and the ache of losing him.

"She has done what she could."

And it was enough. She saw that, saw the comfort her act had brought, for she had seen the burden he bore and in her small way had helped the bearing. No speech marred the stillness now. Hush grew up rich as a golden evening, spiced with the scent of Mary's love. Mary rose, head bowed, and made to escape. At the doorway, Martha stepped suddenly forward and grabbed her sister's hand. Her face was streaked with tears. They left the room together.

Barely a week had passed when Philip stumbled in on Sabbath's eve, breathless with hurry and with the horror of his news. Jesus had been taken by the Sanhedrin. And all was a blur after that, for they rushed out the door with no thought but to be with the Master, to stand by his side. Martha even left her bread rising on the table. They snatched their cloaks and made haste to Jerusalem.

Even as she walked, stumbling on the loose stones of the road, Mary knew in her bones that Jesus' time had come. The time when he must suffer, the time when he must die. They reached Jerusalem in time to see him questioned, to hear Pilate's words ring out and the crowds answer with a death sentence for the man who wanted only to bring them life.

"Crucify him!" they cried.

And once more, Mary sat at the feet of her Lord. She knelt by the foot of the cross, her eyes fixed upon his bloodied face. Her mind could not grasp the horror of this end, the death brought to the Son of God. Yet her soul, even as it ached, felt that the truth of Jesus on the cross was the truth he had taught in her home and on the mountains and in the fields. This end was the truth of love, of One broken to save the world.

If only she could comfort him now.

Then the faintest scent of nard came to her. Could it be that her gift clung yet to his skin, a last fragrance of gentleness in the midst of the hate that destroyed him? She lifted her eyes to his face, and he met her gaze. *Beloved Master*, her soul whispered. *Beloved Mary*, his face said before the pain drove his eyes away.

She had done what she could.

When he died, her heart ripped open, and all that was lovely seemed stricken from the earth. The chief part of her died with him. When she stumbled into Peter's house that night, she felt she could no longer live.

> **A blaze of light streamed from the tomb as they came, like the sun rising after a storm.**

They stayed in Jerusalem through the Sabbath, many of Jesus' followers huddled together in a single room. Martha leaned against Mary and wept. Lazarus looked at Mary with eyes as vacant as on the night he died. When the first morning of the week dawned and they were free to anoint the body, Mary and several other women took linens and spices to honor Jesus one last time.

Through the lifeless streets of sleeping Jerusalem they went, and Mary dragged her feet on the stones, unsure if she could bear the sight of her Lord in death. But she never had to. They reached the tomb and found the mighty stone rolled away. A blaze of light streamed from the tomb as they came, light like the sun rising after a storm, and two men stood suddenly before them. The women knew they were angels—the joy of their faces, the purity of the light that danced in and over and through them spoke of a realm beyond the clutches of the earth.

"Do not be afraid," they said, and Mary thought they seemed like young boys as they laughed. "You are looking for Jesus who died, but he is not here. He is risen, just as he said! Come, see the place where he was laid." And the men beckoned the women to look and see.

The tomb was a tomb in name only, for light cleansed it and washed all scent of death and age from its darkness. The tomb was empty, and the women came out to laugh and weep with the angels.

"Go now," said the men, "tell his disciples that he has risen and is going ahead of them into Galilee. Go in joy!"

They ran, stumbling through Jerusalem in a giddy clatter. John had the door open before they arrived, so loud was their rejoicing. "He is alive!" they shouted and danced in the streets as they had danced on the day that Lazarus was raised.

Mary, flushed with happiness at the news of Jesus' resurrection, stood apart and remembered the miracle of her brother. She thought of the day when Lazarus was raised, remembered the circle of death that Jesus had filled with life. Now, she was certain, all the world would be filled with his light. Death had been turned backwards.

When she saw Jesus later that day, when he came quietly into the place where she sat with her sister, she cried out in joy and hugged him to herself. Many more times in the days to come, he appeared to those who loved him. As if his new life brought mischief with it, he came when they least expected it, now at a feast, now on a walk, now in one of their gatherings on the mountainside. He taught and blessed, he counseled them and answered every question they asked. But soon he would leave, and they all knew it. He would return to the Father he had come to show to the world.

When Jesus called his followers to meet on a mountain outside of Jerusalem, Mary knew that the time had come. She stood, arm linked in Martha's, the wind fresh in her face and the sun gentle on the hills. Hundreds of people stood waiting on the mountain. Jesus stood above them and called down his last command to make disciples of all the earth, and gave his assurance that he would always, always be with them. Mary's gaze was fixed on the kind eyes that first won her heart. Jesus held out his hands. He laughed and suddenly rose like a bird mighty in the sky, and the heavens opened and music beyond the realm of the world came to their ears. And he was gone.

They kept their faces turned upward for a moment, up to the place where beauty and joy reigned free. Then all of them at once, hundreds, turned slowly round and began the walk down. Down into the cities and homes and roads they would walk with the good news of their Lord.

Martha squeezed Mary's arm. "I think we both have the good part now," she laughed, then sniffed.

"We do," said Mary, and she felt Martha's joy and grief in her own heart.

She thought of that night, so long ago now, when she sat at the Master's feet. Mary ached to realize that it might be years before she would see the face of Jesus again. But she would, she knew, when her work here was done. When she had loved as Jesus had loved her, when she had seen and touched the hearts of many lonely people. When she had told as many souls as she could of the one good thing, the priceless gem she had found.

Oh yes, she would sit at his feet again.

And this time, it would be for eternity.

devotional

I am a lover of old art. I cut pictures of masterpieces out of books and frame them. I wander big-city galleries with wide eyes. I love the story a picture tells, because to me, art whispers the history of the heart, the inner secrets people hide behind their eyes. An artist has the unique ability to stop time at a particular moment, to catch the fleeting glance or turn or a moment of beauty that can never quite be caught in real life. In a few, rare pieces, the artist captures a special quality that captivates me like nothing else: quiet.

Quiet. Not stillness, as in lack of motion, nor the languor of repose but, rather, the instant between action and thought, the moment in which a person pauses in sudden meditation. Because of this, some of my favorite paintings are by the Dutch artist Jan Vermeer. One of his works, *Woman Holding a Balance*, painted about 1665, touches me in a particular way. The painting is a simple one, just a young woman in the midst of her daily work. She stands at a table, face awash with sunlight from a small window above her head. She holds a scale in her hands as she measures or counts some simple object. Face gentle, eyes fixed on her work, she is, for that instant, quiet, fully aware of the moment. Poised at the center of that still instant, she watches, she waits, and she ponders.

A moment like that is chosen. A minute more, and she will set the weight down and jot off a number, or hurry to the bread that needs baking or the letter to be written. When I look at the painting, I can almost feel the movement gathering in the scene that lurks just beyond the frame. But the moment of stillness is sacred, and in it the woman sees what is before her with perfect clarity. I think she senses the worth of her work, settles back into the depths of her soul, and is strengthened for the rest of her busy day.

Such quiet takes an action of the will. This is the choice I daily seek in my walk with God. This is the moment I try to make, an instant in which to behold the face of my love, my Lord. Every single morning, I wake up and set about the work of stillness because I believe it is the first thing I must do if I truly want to know Jesus.

Mary did this. Throughout the various Gospel accounts of Mary's interaction with Jesus, the one thing that always stands out to me is her silence. Where Martha is quick to speak, Mary is slow. Martha rushes Jesus with demands for vindication or miracle, but Mary holds back, not in fear but in patience. Her silence is not one of insecurity but is the quiet of a watcher who waits, listens, and perceives.

I believe she understood what drove the heart and actions of her Master because she had made it her life to study him. She sat at his feet and listened while the rest of the world ran crazily about him with a thousand conflicting desires. She cultivated a heart that was open to God. She honed her skills of looking, of listening, of knowing the Master. And in this way, I believe, she was one of the few who understood that Jesus was going to die.

If this is true, it was a remarkable insight on her part. Every common Jewish perception of the promised Messiah was that he would be a victor, a champion of his people. He would conquer the foes of Israel and give his people the safety for which they longed. The crowds and disciples always assumed that someday Jesus would conquer Rome, or at least abash the haughty religious leaders. Again and again, Jesus explained that His kingdom was of heaven, that to bring it to pass He must die. But they were so busy with their own plans they never heard His stated purpose. They did not see the urgency in his eyes.

That is, none except Mary. Her insight allowed her to comfort Him when no one else did, to walk with Him on the hard road that no one else wanted to acknowledge. I believe that all lovers of God are called to be as Mary, to be so deeply aware of God's purposes that we know His heart as she did. But how? It's not as if we modern girls can have Jesus over for dinner like Mary did. We don't have the Messiah sitting at our table, close enough to touch.

Several years ago, I read a book by Evelyn Underhill, a woman who invested a lifetime in studying what it means to contemplate Christ. She wrote:

> Eternity is with us, inviting our contemplation perpetually, but we are too frightened, lazy, and suspicious to respond; too arrogant to still our thought, and let divine sensation have its way. It needs industry and goodwill if we would make that transition; for the process involves a veritable spring-cleaning of the soul, a turning-out and rearrangement of our mental furniture, a wide opening of closed windows, that the notes of the wild birds beyond our garden may come to us fully charged with wonder and freshness, and drown with their music the noise of the gramophone within.[1]

If we want to be as Mary in our own time, I think we must understand that the choice to know God is ours. The Spirit of God is alive and calling out from the very core of our hearts. We have the Bible available to us, and we can offer a prayer at any moment. But the great requirement is that we be still enough to listen. We must hush our hearts every day so that we can learn, hear, and follow.

When I read that passage from Underhill's book, I realized that a cursory, five-minute quiet time would never make me a Mary, nor would a few muttered prayers in between errands. To know the heart of my God would require an investment of myself.

So I started by setting aside five minutes of dedicated prayer each day. I did this in addition to my usual quiet time and slowly worked to ten, then fifteen minutes. I practiced pushing other worries away (and if they would not go, I jotted them down in a notebook to deal with later). I read Scripture or devotional books at certain times each day. I wrote in my journal. I set aside a time when I turned off the computer, phone, iPod, TV, and any other electronic distraction. I tried to remember God throughout my day, to talk with Him as I drove, cooked, or wrote. And slowly, quiet entered into me, and God began to fill my heart.

Oh, don't be fooled—it's always a fight. I struggle every day to keep a quiet heart. We live in a culture so steeped in hurry, so driven by distraction, it's hard for me even to focus my brain on one person or thought at a time. The frenetic modern culture has trained me to seek out noise, to take action, to anything but silence. I cannot count the number of quiet times I have left in utter dejection, sabotaged by my own hyperactive brain. Sometimes I think the closing of my eyes for prayer sets off some inner signal calling every worry, desire, and distraction in my life to mob me all at once.

But I push it all away in my constant determination to see Jesus as Mary saw HIm. I choose quiet again and again and fix my eyes upon Christ. I pick myself up off the floor and try one more time. The reward I seek is a heart with windows flung wide to the wind of God, a soul so quiet that the whisper of God is as music within it. My goal is to be Mary, to be like Vermeer's lovely women, with a heart attuned to all the eternal things that exist beyond the insistent hum of our busy lives. I yearn to see the face of God so clearly that I, like Mary, will work in harmony with His heart and bring Him joy.

Note

1. *Practical Mysticism: A Little Book for Normal People,* Evelyn Underhill (1914).

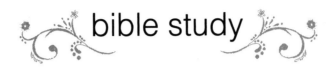

bible study

Psalm 131

To what does the psalmist compare his soul? What has the psalmist refused to do? This psalm was written by King David, ruler, warrior, and father. He must have felt harried every single day. How do you think he cultivated a still heart before God?

1 Kings 19:11–13

When God spoke to Elijah, what did His voice sound like? Do you think God whispers in your own life? Do you hear Him?

1 Peter 3:3–4

Why do you think a gentle and quiet spirit is precious in the sight of God? Do you think this describes Mary? What would it look like in a practical way for you to bring cultivate a quiet spirit in yourself?

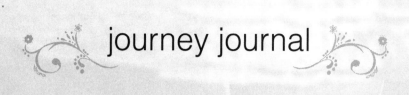

journey journal

chapter four

Story-Formed Soul

"Ah, Mary. Always more questions."

"Always, Abba." Mary grinned at her father as they trod the dusty road home after the Sabbath morning at synagogue.

"What is it this time?" her father asked, eyebrows raised to greet his daughter's usual barrage of inquiry into the meaning of this law or that prophet. Ezekiel had been read aloud in synagogue today.

"A new heart, Abba," she replied, solemnity in the lines of her young face as she looked up. "Ezekiel says that Israel will be given a new heart and made to sin no more. How?"

For an instant there was just the gravelly crunch of their feet, then Mary's father laughed. He shook and rumbled with his mirth, and Mary looked up, puzzled, her mouth crooked with bewildered amusement.

"Oh, my Mary," her father breathed between his laughter, "You like the impossible ones, don't you? You ask questions I cannot answer. Well," and he forced himself into a serious tone, "he will give us a new heart. How? I don't know. But Isaiah tells us it is the Messiah on whom all our hopes rest. Somehow, this promised one of God will take away the sin of his people. It is the Messiah who is the answer, though we have yet to see how. And that's the best I can do for now. Are you satisfied, Mary?"

She nodded and sidled closer to her father.

He grinned down at his daughter, his fondness for her lighting his eyes. Mary was small, a simple girl beautified by the grace of a kindled spirit. Again, as he had a hundred times since her birth, he thought that if she had been born a man, she would have made a fine rabbi. But Yahweh knew best. Mary would be a wife and mother as all good Jewish women were, and perhaps Joseph, her betrothed, would enjoy having his ear talked off. Even her impossible questions were always so sweetly asked.

"Mary!" Father and daughter both perked at the call from up the road and looked to see Mary's mother leaning out the doorway of their house. "Hurry up, love. I'm desperate for help with the meal."

Mary squeezed her father's hand and scurried up the road, waving at her father just before she disappeared. Her Abba waved back and smiled for the joy of having such a daughter. He was glad, he decided, to settle his jewel on Joseph. A better man could not be found for his thoughtful daughter. For Joseph loved the Torah as Mary did, and he would value the soul of the girl-woman just as her father had before him. An ache came into his heart at thought of the loss he must soon face. A jewel among women, his Mary.

Dust sifted through the gold light of late afternoon as Mary ambled, tired and glad, to the circle of trees in the far corner of her father's fields. Bread baking and meal making and the rounds of work that crafted a home could be exhausting. Yet the glow of it filled her, for it was all practice for the life she soon would share with Joseph. Once again she blessed God for giving her such a husband.

She settled herself against a small cedar and leaned back so that the light fell in dappled play over her face. The sun's warmth pooled golden around her, and quiet settled on her head. Easy, she thought, to love God when his goodness was so plain in her life. She closed her eyes and wondered. What if she could truly see all the goodness of God, the height and depth of it? Maybe, she thought, if a person could stare long enough at the loveliness of God, it would enter in and make him new. Maybe blindness made people struggle as they did, and new sight would restore them. The words of the psalmist played in her mind: *One thing I have asked . . . to behold the beauty of the Lord.*

The scratch of a step in the nearby grass jolted her from her thoughts. She opened her eyes, expecting to see Joseph. But a stranger stood before her instead, and her breath caught. Never had she seen a human whose beauty struck her as a light upon her face, whose presence caused music to thrum in her soul. As if God met the desire of her thoughts and presented a reflection of his unutterable beauty, this man walked out of her mind with eyes deep as a storm sky, his face like the morning in its youth.

"Greetings, favored one, the Lord is with you," he said.

Mary fell back, bewildered. Favored one? Favored of God? A common girl in a dusty village with the glory days of Israel a forgotten dream? She knew herself to be sinful and young and full of the loves of the earth. How could she have pleased the Almighty? But who, then, was this man who was like God and yet not? Fear tinged her confusion and she tensed, unsure of how to meet this shifting of the borders between spirit and earth.

"Don't be afraid, Mary." His voice was gentle, his face kind. "For you have found favor with God."

She did not answer, and he was silent a moment, looking kindly down upon her as she tried with all her might to understand the words he said and the cause for his coming. Then he opened his arms wide and flung his next words to the height of heaven and the unknown depths of the earth and all the wild pathways of her soul. His voice gathered to a brightness now and rang like a bell through Mary's heart.

"For behold, you will conceive in your womb and bear a son, and you shall call his name Jesus. He will be great, and he will be called the Son of the Most High, and the Lord God will give him the throne of his father David, and he will reign over the house of Jacob forever." Now the words became as stars that leapt across the heavens, as trumpets announcing creation. "And of his kingdom there shall be no end!"

Suddenly she knew: This man was an angel of the Lord, and it was the Messiah of whom he spoke. The coming king who would save his people. The beloved leader for whom the prophets cried and the lowly people, like Mary herself, yearned. The Messiah was coming, and she was somehow to play a part in introducing him to the world.

All her life, Mary had listened to the laments of the prophets who called for God to deliver them. All her life, Mary had held up her heart in faith to the Lord, to the God of her people whose salvation she hoped to someday see. Now, as the fact of his coming was trumpeted in this place, she was filled with wonder. However, she had one, quite urgent question.

"How will this be, since I am a virgin?"

Amusement brought tenderness to the eyes of the angel as he looked down at Mary and saw a young human girl, like all others, concerned with the details of how God's fathomless glory would invade the workaday minutes of her life. He bent forward and was gentle as he said to her, "The Holy Spirit will come upon you, and the Spirit of the Most High will overshadow you, and for that reason, the holy child will be called the Son of God. Behold, even your relative Elizabeth has conceived a son in her old age, and she who was barren is now in her sixth month."

To Mary's shock, the angel knelt and peered into her face, his hands open before him as if to offer her some gift. And he said, "For nothing is impossible with God."

God was to be the father of her child, and that child was Messiah. Joy and terror tore at her soul, for she was unworthy, yet chosen. Frightened, yet filled with awe. Tears came then in shocked elation that, for a moment, stole words from Mary's mouth. She knew only that God's love had come to her, and she determined to submit. She lifted her face to the angel and said, "I am the servant of the Lord. May it be to me just as you have said."

And there was laughter, a shout of joy all around her, as the angel received the brave answer of the woman chosen to bear God's greatest gift into existence on the earth. Mary thought the voice of the angel brightened the blue of the sky, set the grass to waving, the wind to a whirl. In that moment, it was as if all creation leaned toward her and the angel to share their joy, to watch the story unfold. Then, in a shout of laughter, the glory of the angel gathered itself together, and in a last burst of light he was gone.

> **It was as if all creation leaned toward them to share their joy.**

For a while, all was still. Mary savored the joy that echoed in the air about her. And she waited. Dusk swathed the fields in shadow while the sun set itself ablaze in a death fire above. When the darkness had grown to a purple velvet and the shout of the light reached its last triumph, God came. She felt him as a deepening of the silence, the sudden leaping of every cell in her body to honor the presence of the One who was the source of all life. She closed her eyes and knelt. She prostrated herself on the grass, stretched out her hands on the earth of which her body was made and honored the Maker of it all.

And the Spirit of God overshadowed the humble girl who awaited him. The glory of the Most High limited itself to fit within the body of a woman who received him with a glad, willing heart. And the miracle of Jesus began.

Night cloaked Mary as she walked home, trying to think what to say to her family. At first, she thought her family would hear her tale with just the same awe and wonder she felt. But as she rehearsed the words in her mind, she realized swiftly that it is no easy thing to tell of a visit from God Most High— especially when the news included a baby that was not the child of the man to whom she was betrothed.

She decided she would tell her father first. The cold night air pricked her skin and drove her toward the barn where her father was working. She sighed. She would just have to speak what came to her heart.

"Abba?" she called.

He grunted assent and did not look up.

Her news ached and swelled with her. "Abba, I need to speak with you."

He turned from his work, eyebrows lifted at the urgency of her tone. Curiosity kindled in his eyes. "You have a light about you Mary," he said, "yet you are troubled. You look almost afraid. Come, sit with me here, sit down my child."

He led her gently to a low ledge in the stable. Hay scratched at her skin and scented the air with its dust. The donkey kicked a little and brayed in the corner. Whispering comfort, the small sounds and smells of the stable rose to Mary, familiar as her own breath. She settled against her father as he sat down.

"Abba, you remember the question I asked you today? About sin? And you said that the Messiah would be the answer, even if you didn't know how?"

"Yes, my Mary, yes. What does this have to do with us right now?"

Mary laughed and then tensed. "Well, Abba. I don't know how to say it. I don't know how to help you believe me. But Abba," she hesitated, then spat it out with abandon, "I saw an angel today. I was in the field, and an angel of God came to me and told me the Messiah is coming."

She saw laughter rise in her father's eyes then fade as the tears in her own convinced him she was in earnest. Her father leaned back and let out of a breath of astonishment. Mary was not a teaser. She had ever been sweet and earnest, full of joy, but not mischievous.

"Who came to you? How did it happen? And why you, Mary?"

Finally, here was something she could answer with ease. With the art of a born storyteller, she wove the tale of the bright angel and his ringing words. But when she came to the news of a baby to be born, her father stood up and very nearly stomped.

"Mary, are you mad?"

She knew it sounded outlandish. Yet what was God but a great, sweet mystery to his people? Silent, she watched her father pace and prayed that he would believe her. But when he turned to face her, she cringed at the suspicion in his eyes.

"Mary, has any man . . . ? Has Joseph . . . ? If you are with child because of another's sin . . ." Her father's knuckles went white from the grasp he had of the stable ledge. "Mary, I will not be angry. But virgins do not have children!"

"One virgin will," she countered and stood, eyes in a sudden blaze. "The one of whom Isaiah spoke. Is it so impossible to believe that I am she? Abba, I am that woman. I am the chosen of God. I am unworthy—surely everyone is unworthy—but Messiah is coming and he is coming through me. Abba . . ." Her voice broke with fear at the distance that had suddenly opened between her and the man who had always been her protector. "Abba, please. He said nothing is impossible with God. You can test what I have said. The angel told me that Aunt Elizabeth is also with child. Please believe me."

> **"Messiah is coming, and he is coming through me."**

Her father laughed then, a laugh robbed of joy, a laugh ugly for its fear.

"Elizabeth with child? Mary, you're dreaming. I think you've gone mad."

Now Mary stood. "Abba, have you ever known me to lie? Have I ever sought to trick you, to tell you wild stories? What I speak is true. Yes, it is outlandish and shocking. It is a thing of fear and a thing of joy. But, Abba, I think that is always the way of it when God confronts his people. He is so far above us, we cannot help bewilderment when he comes to us. And yet he is coming. You will see."

She pulled her arms around herself as if to draw peace to her heart and hold it there. Straight as a young tree, quiet as the night around her, she stood, and there was a strength in her stance that belied her youth. She would wrangle no more, and her father knew it.

"Well," he sighed, "I have always trusted you before, and that is the reason I will not pursue this further now. But you are to tell no one, do you understand? Not even your mother. At least, not until I decide what to do. Let us go in."

Had Isaiah met with such skepticism? In the days the followed, Mary thought he must have. Never before had she considered the challenge of getting your own people to believe that you have heard from God. As the child stirred to life in her body, as her father watched her with shrewd eyes, the words of the prophets gave Mary strength. When on the next Sabbath the rabbi read Isaiah's words that a virgin would conceive a child and give him a name that means "God with us," Mary bit her tongue hard to keep the tears of pain and gladness from making a fool of her before the entire village.

Two more weeks passed. Mary waited, speaking to no one of what had happened. Conversation with her father was strained. And then one day, he called to her.

"Mary!" His voice was sharp, and she straightened from her digging in the garden. She found him just out the door of the house, hands on his hips, watching a caravan retreat down the road.

"Abba, you called me?" Mary shielded her eyes from the sun and waited.

For a moment, he did not answer, his gaze focused in the far distance, beyond the caravan, beyond the horizon. He jerked back to the present at her touch and peered down at her. A glad shock thrilled in her at the gentleness rekindled in his eyes.

"Well, you'll never believe the news I've had. Or, well, I suppose you will. I'm the one who can't account for it. That caravan brought word from Zechariah and Elizabeth." He stopped and took a breath, looking so little-boyishly bewildered that Mary wanted to laugh as he shrugged his shoulders and said, "Elizabeth is to bear a child. Just as you said."

Mary resisted the urge to prance about and laugh. Instead, she threw her arms about her father and beamed. This was grace to her as well as him, another miracle to affirm the first.

"I feel, Mary," he said, his voice weakened by a hesitancy Mary had never heard before, "I feel that I walk in a dream. That miracles and puzzlements dog me, not as joy, but as things that make me afraid. Have all men felt this way when God spoke to them? I believe you Mary because I have no choice. But it brings me no joy."

He drew her aside from the open door, fearing they might be overheard.

"I am afraid for you, my daughter. I am afraid for what will happen when this thing becomes known. Many will judge you, and I hope you will be strong enough to bear all that comes. This is why I have decided you should visit Elizabeth. I arranged with the caravan that just left to escort you to her home on their way back to the hill country. I don't know how to believe, but it's all happening whether I do or no. Perhaps Elizabeth can tell you more. Your journey begins in two days."

Elizabeth patted her belly. "Well, little one, it's just you and me." Strange, she thought, how in all her years she had imagined that children would shatter the silence of her solitude. Yet the coming of a child prodded her to a quiet she had never known. Six months now she had spent largely secluded. Zechariah could not speak, and she did not need to. The baby burgeoning within her had been company enough.

Today, though, she had been restless. So she sat out of doors, enjoying the warm wind but sheltered from the sun by the trees clustered at the corners of her house. The baby was restless too, squirming and kicking at her.

When she spotted a slight figure rounding the bend of the road, Elizabeth sat straighter and shaded her eyes. Her heart stirred as if to meet something her spirit and child had already expected.

"Elizabeth?" The young woman's greeting was hesitant yet eager as it floated up the wind to where Elizabeth waited. "It's Mary, Anna's daughter."

At that moment, the baby leapt in her womb as if in wild answer, and Elizabeth was filled, body and soul, with the Holy Spirit. God opened her eyes to the miracle that had filled Mary, and Elizabeth knew that the mother of the Messiah had spoken. She was filled with a swell of exultation, and she laughed at the thought that salvation was walking up the road to greet her. Elizabeth stood and ran, large and bumbling as she was, and caught the girl in her arms.

"Blessed are you among women," she panted, "and blessed is the child you bear!"

Then, pushing Mary a little back so that she could see her eyes, she put her wrinkled, old woman's hands around the young face and asked, "But why am I so favored that the mother of my Lord should visit me? As soon as the sound of your voice reached my ears, the baby inside me leapt for joy!"

Mary began weeping, sudden and silent, and Elizabeth knew with pierced heart how much this girl must have borne. Her journey must have been wearying, and no doubt her parents were bewildered by the miracle of her pregnancy. Yet here she was, filled with the grace of God.

"Oh, Mary," she said, wiping the tears from the girl's face, "blessed are you for believing that God would fulfill his promises to you."

At her words, Mary's tears ceased. There was such joy in Mary's face that Elizabeth stepped back as if from the blaze of a holy fire.

Then Mary lifted her face and cried aloud:

"My soul glorifies the Lord,
and my spirit rejoices in God my Savior,
for he has been mindful of the
humble state of his servant.
From now on all generations will call me blessed,
for the Mighty One has done great things for me—
holy is his name.

His mercy extends to those who fear him,
from generation to generation.
He has performed mighty deeds with his arm;
he has scattered those who are proud in their inmost thoughts.

He has brought down rulers from their thrones
but has lifted up the humble.
He has filled the hungry with good things
but has sent the rich away empty.
He has helped his servant Israel,
remembering to be merciful
to Abraham and his descendants forever,
just as he said to our fathers."

The words of prophets were echoed in Mary's song. This was the yearning of the psalmists, the long, aching history of a people waiting for Messiah. Elizabeth marveled that the words of this young girl revealed a heart steeped in the story of her God, a heart rejoicing at the salvation of the Lord she had long trusted. God knew, thought Elizabeth. He knew just whom to choose to be the mother of his Son.

devotional

Why did God choose Mary?

I think most Christian women ask this question at some point in their life because, after all, she was selected to be God's mother. Whatever she did, or was, must have been God's ideal, and all of us hope to be just that. Yet her qualities as recorded in the Bible remain a bit elusive. She was young, she was willing, and she was betrothed. We're not given much historical detail beyond that, and I always assumed that Mary must have just been a little more perfect than the rest of us.

That is, until I studied the song known as the Magnificat. When we take a close look at the mighty psalm of praise that Mary spoke the day she came to Elizabeth, we can understand why she was qualified for this honor. In the words of her song we see a vital quality that set Mary apart from most other women in the world: She knew the story of her God.

Read the words of her song and you realize this was a woman who knew the law and prophets with a lover's comprehension and a scholar's zeal. She was probably curious, her heart open to the Word of God as it was read on the Sabbath. I like to imagine that she questioned her elders and memorized the psalms, hiding the words of the prophets in her pondering heart. The Magnificat is the lyrical, jubilant cry of a woman who knew the words of God as if they were her own.

Think of the prophets and psalms she alludes to in her song:

My soul glorifies the Lord (Hannah's song in 1 Samuel 2)

and my spirit rejoices in God my Savior (Habakkuk 3:18)

for he has been mindful of the

humble state of his servant. (Psalm 138:6)
From now on all generations will call me blessed,
for the Mighty One has done great things for me—
(Psalm 50:1)
holy is his name. (Isaiah 6:3)
His mercy extends to those who fear him,
from generation to generation. (Psalm 103:17)
He has performed mighty deeds with his arm; (Psalm 98:1)
he has scattered those who are proud in their inmost
thoughts.
He has brought down rulers from their thrones
but has lifted up the humble. (Job 5:11)
He has filled the hungry with good things (Psalm 107:9)
but has sent the rich away empty.
He has helped his servant Israel,
remembering to be merciful (Psalm 78:37)
to Abraham and his descendants forever,
just as he said to our fathers. (Genesis 22:16–18)

Mary knew the story of God. She knew the history of his people and the promises he'd made. Because of that, she didn't crumple in shock when the angel came with his startling news. She knew that the prophets had foretold a child born to a virgin, that this child was the promised Messiah who would save His people. Mary was able to say "May it be to me just as you have said" because she knew the story to which she was being called.

It's the same story we are all called to join.

Not long ago, I wrote a book on the subject of children's literature. Part of my research included studying how stories affect children. Not only how words build their brains, but also how stories shape their souls. Reading stories helps people to understand themselves as heroes or heroines in a tale of their own. Children are far more ready to be brave, imaginative, and full of wonder if they have dwelt in a storybook world where giants are fought and princesses won and great adventures undertaken. I think God created us to be people whose hearts are quickened by a good tale.

I also think God meant Scripture to be the story we live, the epic in which we are immersed. God's story is the one great, true story of the world, as wild and woven with mystery as the myths and legends and fairy tales of old. In it we are the knights and fair maidens, the Davids and Esthers and Daniels that people His story. But only those who know and love and live the story of God will be aware of the part they have been called to play.

If you want to be a Mary, a true-hearted woman of God, you must immerse yourself in Scripture. Daily reading of the Bible is the bedrock foundation of a Christ-centered life. And I don't mean reading one verse then scurrying off to breakfast. I mean a study of God's Word, a day-by-day enrichment of your soul. One of the prophets described it this way: "God wakens me morning by morning" (Isaiah 50:4).

The godliest women I know all share a daily Bible study in common. When my mentor, Phyllis, had just become a Christian, she decided she would read a little of God's Word every day. Fifty years later, she keeps this promise. I have traveled with Phyllis, stayed in her home, and witnessed her very busy life. During one lovely jaunt to Prince Edward Island, I came out of my room every morning to find her with a Bible open on her lap as the sun rose. When we came back in the afternoon from a tiring outing, she'd pick it up again, peruse a Psalm, or ponder something Jesus said. Scripture is now such a part of her thoughts that when we talk, her words echo with prophets' cries and psalmists' songs. Her conversation is peppered with references to God's love, His vision for His people, His care in all circumstances. Phyllis is a Mary in my time, and this is what I think God wants every girl to be.

I have always tried to read my Bible most days, but two years ago I did something I had never done. Inspired by Phyllis and other women in my life, I chose to tackle one of the prophets from first word to last. If God wanted me to read His Word, I was going to do it with vim. I chose Isaiah and studied each line with a scholar's care. The funny thing was that I did it as a long-distance participant in a Bible study in Kentucky.

One blustery Saturday in the spring of that year, I visited my study friends and spent an afternoon with the leader of the group (and one of my dearest friends). I must have had a hundred and three questions about Isaiah, and I think I asked most of them that day. Rain-drenched light poured in a bay window over the table where we sat with coffee, Bibles and notebooks open, pens in hand. For three luminous hours, we talked through Isaiah. At the end of it, I remember sitting back in my spindle-legged chair, that pure, grey light in my eyes and a light just as serene in my spirit. I grasped the epic, world-encompassing story of God that day in a way I never had.

This is the gift of a Mary heart, the understanding that comes to a mind that sets itself on knowing the story of God. Scripture opened my eyes to God's work throughout history, to His faithfulness and love. Though I was not quite a Mary, I was at least ready to take up my part in His drama.

God didn't choose Mary because she was beautiful or perfect or better at housework than the other village girls. She was simply the one who was ready. Mary was chosen because her heart had already embraced the story of God. She was ready to be a heroine. I hope I am too.

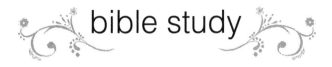

bible study

Psalm 1

What do you think it means to meditate on God's Word day and night? Why would you choose His law as the subject of your meditation in place of other things? Why do you think His words bring such life?

Psalm 119:49–56

How does knowing the story of God bring us hope and strength? What does it mean to carry Scripture as the "song" of your heart throughout your life?

Isaiah 50:4–5

What do you think it means to have the "tongue of a disciple" (or an ear or heart)? What do you think you can do to create this in your life? Do you think God is willing to whisper His story to you?

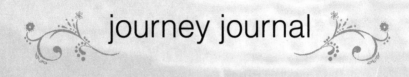

journey journal

chapter five

Swords and Starlight

Mary was having the dream again. She whimpered in the thick shadows and wrapped her arms round herself, trying to shield her heart from the terror she knew would come. In her dream she tensed in anticipation of the pain she knew would descend any moment. And it did. The swift, merciless stab out of the darkness, a knife in her heart that left her gasping for breath. Tears came to her eyes, panic to her throat. She flailed her arms and cried out. Then she woke.

Breath heaving as if she had been running, she sat up from her thin pallet by the campfire and put her hand to her heart. The open sky stretched above the farmer's field, the campfire sizzling low beside her. Mary fell back, limp with relief to be awake. But her peace did not last, for soon came the usual ache, keener than the fear of her dream. Quietly as she could so as not to wake her Joseph, she wept. The knife in her dream was nothing more than the truth of the pain she bore each day.

Joseph's face, that was the first cut. The mere memory of his eyes still hurt her, the way the kind light of his gaze slowly blackened when she told him the news. Mary had stayed with Elizabeth three months, and when she returned her belly had barely swollen. If she wore loose clothing, the miracle child was hidden. She sent for Joseph the moment she returned, for she wanted him to hear the marvelous truth from her own lips and share her joy. Ah, she was fresh with hope then. Elizabeth's firm faith, the months spent in a household marked by miracle, these had buoyed Mary's hope. She returned to Nazareth certain she could convince everyone she loved of the truth.

Joseph came swiftly in answer to her summons, merry with relief at his beloved's return. He patted the heads of Mary's younger siblings, laughed aloud, and pounded her father on the back. Then he and Mary had walked into the garden, hand in hand. She spoke of the prophets, made him remember their many talks of Messiah, for they both were lovers of Torah. And then, her voice low, she told him of all that had passed and how it was with her.

A sudden dark came into his kindly eyes. He dropped his face and sat on the ground. Mary knelt, heart in a panic, and pleaded. She saw that he heard nothing of the miracle. She fell silent, watching hurt fill him until he bent double.

"With child?" he breathed. "My Mary with another man's child? If you had not told me, I would never believe it." Then came the flash of anger, of faith broken, of fear that filled his face. "Who's the father?" he bellowed. "Mary, who else is there? I thought I knew you."

"Joseph," she cried, "you know me to my very soul. This is God's child, I tell you."

He had pushed her off then. Shoved her hand from his, stood and stared at her, his eyes fierce in the darkness. "At least tell me the truth. Mary, you could be stoned for this. I could never cause that, for I have loved you. But at least you could have told me the truth and left the Scripture sacred. I never thought you a liar."

Into the night he stumbled and left her—left her as sky and soul crashing down about her. Up until then, doubt had been something she could fight. But this wound was struck before she could shield herself and would not be mended.

Then came the stab of rejection. Joseph was merciful—he divorced her quietly, but it was news to all the neighbors by nightfall. Soon the child could no longer be hidden. Without a word, Mary was cut off from the community. She received no invitations to feast or share the joy of harvest. The girls who had been Mary's companions since childhood now forsook her, and when they met in the street, it was as if their friendship had never been. Even Hannah, the dearest friend of Mary's youth, shunned her, though she at least came to say good-bye, late one night when no one could see. Both girls wept, clinging together, knowing that when they parted they might not speak again.

Mary could no longer visit the well during the busy morning time for fear of the cold faces she would meet. Nor could she worship or hear the words for which her soul yearned at synagogue, for the anger on the faces of the men frightened even her father. In the eyes of her village, Mary was the worst kind of woman, careless of her family, her husband, and the honor of her people. An adulteress.

All this Mary bore mostly in silence. Only with her father—her lone, reluctant believer—did she weep. With the others, she bore the

> **All this Mary bore mostly in silence.**

hurt with a quiet that stymied them. She took the blows of accusation and silence and would not respond. Yet a tempest sometimes screamed in her heart, a wild raging against the loss of all she had loved. At such times, she often crept away to be alone. Out in the place where the angel came, she lifted her face to God and sought to accept that to bear this baby meant the loss of all she had known.

Then one day, when the sky was a gray veil and the air smoky with rain, she sat against the tree where the angel had found her and pondered. How rash her answer had been that day! Not for a moment did she stop and think what the words might cost her. Knowing now, would she answer the same again? The question echoed in her heart and mind. She rocked back and forth and strove to make the answer the same as on that wondrous day.

"Mary, Mary!"

The voice plunged into her thoughts, and she put a hand to her heart.

Joseph was coming, crashing across the field, leaping the ruts like a small boy, his voice high and his face full of joy. She barely had time to stand before he was there, gasping for breath. He lifted her and held her so tight that she laughed and squirmed for breath. He loved her, he claimed her! Without his speaking a word, she knew.

"Mary, an angel came to me too!" Joseph's face beamed as if it were the greatest honor in the world. "He told me all about your baby. He said it was holy and that I should take you for my wife."

He set her on her feet and grabbed her hands.

"We're getting married. Now. And we're going to make a feast of it. But, Mary, first," he dropped her hands and wrung his together in woeful anguish, "can you ever forgive me? You were heart of my heart, and I rejected you. Can you forgive me?"

Her answer was a hand on his face and gentle eyes so full of joy they shimmered in the dusk. They walked home hand in hand, planning a wedding feast for two days hence. Joseph insisted that it be a joyous, extravagant thing. The rest of the town could hide in their houses, he said, but he was to be bridegroom to the most wonderful woman in the world. God obviously agreed, he whispered.

So the families of Joseph and Mary celebrated, laughed heartily, largely ignoring the bump under Mary's bridal tunic, and sang as if it were the wedding of a princess. And for a little while, there was joy.

A few months later, soldiers rode into the village and proclaimed a census of the whole Roman world, ordering every man to return to the town of his fathers. Joseph was of the line of David, in the town of Bethlehem, a four-day journey from Nazareth. At first, the family argued that Mary should remain behind to give birth, for she was very near her time. But Joseph fought them, and Mary yielded. The angel had appointed Joseph as father to the holy child, and Mary would go where he went.

But to leave, forced from her home, to watch her family stand bent-shouldered in the dawn, this caused a ripping deep in Mary's soul. Of all the sorrows she had known or would in years to come, that leaving of her family was among the worst. Especially the parting from her mother, whose life had made her own and whose kindness had shaped her to love. Her mother did not understand the miracle, and Mary had no comfort to offer her. Her first child would be born in a strange place far from her family.

Joseph and Mary left at dawn one day, and Mary could not speak over her tears until the sun had traveled half the sky.

Now she lay on her back by the campfire, squirming. Never could she quite get her bones into a comfortable position these days. Joseph slept beside her, exhausted by the day's travel. She ought to sleep, too, but sorrow hollowed out her middle. The dream had laid her heart bare, and sleep fled before it. She lay there haunted.

Where was God, the Father of this child, whose face she could not see? She carried the treasure of the universe in her womb, yet the universe buffeted her about like a bird caught in a storm. She never supposed that to be God's chosen meant the luxurious life of a queen, yet surely it meant protection. God, she once thought, would guard her from the anguish of hurting the family she loved. Surely God would allow his child to enter this world surrounded by an extended family who would love and protect him.

Instead, here she was, on her way to a city she did not know and with no idea where she was to give birth. To follow God, she had found, was to walk in darkness.

How then, she asked, do any stay faithful? How did Moses, Job, and Hosea stay in love with the God who had cost them so much? Tears came again as she lay, too weak to resist her despair, too tired to reach for faith.

An arm slipped about her then.

Joseph. Strong and warm, a bulk of protection at her back.

"My Mary, I am so sorry. I would do anything to bear the pain you feel."

"Joseph," she choked, "why do I feel like this? I think I could bear it if God would come closer, if he seemed nearer. I am willing to follow him. I am. But I can't feel him anymore. We have lost so much. And I am in darkness."

For some moments, silence fell between them as her own words echoed in her mind. *Why, why, why?*

"Mary," Joseph whispered, "when I was in doubt all those weeks, when the hurt of losing you burned in my soul, I went many nights out into the fields. At first, I never looked up. I saw only the blackness of my despair. I could not bring myself even to look at the stars."

"Joseph," Mary asked, her eyes closed against the night, "why do the righteous suffer? Why did you have to wait in doubt for the angel? If we are obedient to Yahweh, surely he should protect us."

> **"To struggle is part of life in this world."**

"I have no answer for that. I don't know why God seems far away, or why he has taken us on this journey, or why you, the very mother of his child, must suffer." His voice echoed with a note of the grief he had felt on the night he left Mary, thinking himself betrayed. "I think this earth is a dark place. The whole world is veiled in a black night, and even when we love God, we still live among the shadows. To struggle is part of life in this world."

It was a truth she did not want to hear but one that rang true to every ache of her heart. She wanted her obedience to God to guarantee her joy, to shield her from loneliness and doubt. How could she go on if there was only more pain to come?

Joseph reached suddenly for her hand and said, "Look up, Mary!"

Turning her face to the night sky, her gaze was filled with starlight. The stars glimmered in an everlasting dance, thick and misty in one corner of the sky, diamond-cut brilliant in another. The light fell upon her face like the eyes of God.

"The stars, Mary, they are like hope." Joseph's voice now was strangely golden, full of a surety that shook Mary from the languor of her grief. "These tiny, stubborn lights shine on the darkest of nights. It took me weeks before I could make myself look to heaven when I lost you, but slowly I did. Night by night, I began to watch the stars, and the light gave me hope."

Eyes fixed on the sky, Mary held Joseph tightly and her heart took a tiny step toward hope. As if he felt the yielding of her grief, Joseph sat up and pulled Mary up beside him. Lifting his arm, he pointed to this star or that, this gathering of light, that cloud of glory. And as her eyes darted back and forth through the heavens, he faced her and held her hands.

"Mary," he said, voice low and strong, "cling to that light. Do not despair. God will be good to us, even when we cannot see how he is helping us. I learned that in my nights in the fields. The clouds of my despair did not change the goodness of God's plan. But the stars helped me to remember. They light even the blackest night. And, my Mary, morning is coming. Morning always comes in the end. You must hold to that. And count the stars we can see."

Mary sighed, feeling for a brief instant that she was a child being cajoled. But Joseph's words wove a cord of hope to which she clung, willing her heart to respond. She would hold onto the many small graces of God as stars in the night of her despair. She took a very deep breath and let Joseph see the light come back to her eyes.

"I will try. I'll keep looking up, if you'll help me."

In the long, hot days that followed, she remembered to watch for the stars of God. She counted the small kindnesses of an old woman who offered her a cup of water. She counted each warm meal a grace, each shelter a gift. When they reached Bethlehem and her time came upon her, she counted it grace when they found a small stable where she could be settled and safe. Her baby was born with the help of a fat, good-natured midwife who clucked and comforted.

And when Mary held her baby in her arms, when the light of the world and the mercy of God was a squirming child in her hands, the light was so bright she could not speak for its beauty. Morning had come to her heart and to the whole world. The sweetness of this baby in her arms was a joy like no other. Light of her heart, star of his people, bringer of dawn.

The temple was a bustling place, abuzz with voices high and low, sharp and sweet, and filled with the scents of sacrifice and food. The sounds echoed from the richly carved temple pillars. Mary and Joseph walked through it all as though it were a dream. The baby they carried was the Son of God, and this was his house. Mary laughed often at the sheer wonder of it. After they made their small sacrifice and the priest blessed their baby, they were ready to go. But suddenly, from the mulling crowd about them, a wiry hand grasped Mary's arm. An old man stood before them, nearly jumping up and down with excitement.

"I know this baby," he whispered, his face bright as a child's though creased with long years, his eyes on Jesus' little face as if the baby were his own. "You hold the Messiah."

Mary and Joseph both gasped.

"How do you know that?" stammered Mary.

"For many years I have prayed for the salvation of Israel. Then the Holy Spirit came to me and told me I would not die until I had seen the salvation of God. And here he is, beautiful baby boy."

Simeon held out his arms, eyes begging Mary to let him hold the child he had waited all his life to see. She gave him Jesus and was glad, for her own hands trembled. Simeon gazed at the child, and Mary saw the beauty of morning light rising in his face. But then a keen stare came into his old eyes, and he looked at Mary and Joseph, speaking a prophecy over the holy child and a song to the God who sent him:

"Oh Lord, now let me, your servant, depart in peace, for my eyes have seen your salvation, the goodness you have prepared for all people. A light to the Gentiles, and the glory of your people, Israel."

With hands gnarled by age and shaking with emotion, Simeon placed the child back in Mary's arms. He set his hand on the baby's head and blessed the most beautiful thing he had ever seen. But then he turned to

Mary, and the joy was gone from his face, replaced by a razor-sharp gleam that pierced her heart. He put his hand on her arm and spoke.

"This child will cause many to rise and fall in Israel. He has been sent as a sign from God, but many will oppose him."

Mary felt that Simeon suddenly opened a door to the darkest room of her heart and peered in where the blackness of night, the anguish of her dream, still lingered. This was her fear, the dark terror that her child would suffer. That he would struggle, that he would be harmed. As if Simeon could see this plainly in her eyes, he looked on her and spoke the words that would haunt her the rest of her life:

"A sword will pierce your own soul too."

Standing there, she could almost feel the sword's thrust in her fight to obey God. The stab of it was in the memory of every face that had turned from her, in the loss of her home and family. This was the sword of pain, the knife of suffering that stabbed the hearts of those who followed God. She could not escape pain in this dark world. She dropped her eyes, unable to sustain Simeon's stare.

Jesus yawned and blinked, catching her eye. His eyes were glossy with sleep, his sweet, small mouth open. Her heart almost broke, for she began to understand: Her child would bear the worst wound of all—his heart would be broken. Though she could not yet speak it, she knew that her son was born to suffer. To bear, to fight, to pay a great price in the saving of his people. The sword would come worst to her, she knew, when this baby was struck by the world he came to make right.

But this had be the way of it. This son in her arms was the Son of God come to bear the pain of his people. The great beauty of the ages lay as a baby in her hands, and he would be broken to heal the fallen world. This was the way of all lovers of light, all followers of God. Grief is the price to be paid for faith in a broken world. But could she bear it?

Simeon took her hand, and his touch coaxed her to meet his gaze again. His was a face aged with waiting, etched by the yearning that formed and drove his thoughts through all the years of his life. He had grown bent and frail in his long watch for God's Messiah. But now his face shone with the vigor of youth. Hope had come to Simeon. He gripped Mary's hand hard and passed his hope to her. He lay his hand upon her head and blessed her. He shut the door to the dark place within her and drew her with him beyond, into a realm where all things were possible. The starlight came back to her heart.

"The glory of his people, Israel."

Mary gripped Simeon's hand and looked free into his eyes as he blessed her.

devotional

"For that glory, I will bear it," she said.

I had forty-five hours of drive time and two weeks of road trip under my belt by the time I reached Boston. My brother Joel, a student there, planned to meet me for the day so we could explore downtown. We had schemed up quite an industrious tour of Boston history, but when the day came and we met early that morning at the train station, he looked just as tired as I felt. We lounged, wan and sleepy on a bench, and wondered if we should even try.

We were both as tired in soul as we were in body. Midterm finals and questions about his future did it for him. I, on the other hand, had been wrestling over questions and problems that God simply would not answer. I was lonely, exhausted, and dreading the journey home with no certain plan to greet me there. We didn't say it, but both of us felt shaky in our faith, bewildered as to where God was in the midst of our hectic lives.

But as we sat there, an idea struck me out of the morning blue. "Joel," I said, feeling that I had come upon the answer to some impossible question, "let's get out of town. Let's drive up to Concord where the leaves are turning and all those old writers used to live. Let's escape!" So entirely on impulse, we bundled into my car and drove away from the city and into a maze of tiny roads winding around village greens, with prim, pale houses lining the way. The day couldn't have been clearer or the sapphire sky brighter. We parked in the heart of a glad little village, found a coffee shop with excellent cappuccinos and raspberry rugelach, then went on a tour of Louisa May

Alcott's childhood home.

It's no wonder Louisa May grew up to write such famous books. The Alcotts were a family of idealists. She was raised by a father who believed in providing his children a living education through literature, long walks, and discussion round the clock. Joel and I came out eyes widened with new ideas. We found a tiny, wood-floored cottage grocery where we bought a baguette, cheese, and a ripe pear, then headed for the shores of Thoreau's Walden Pond.

Some golden grace took hold of our hours and stretched our afternoon to such a length of peace, we felt like different people at the end. We ate first, perched on a stone wall, with Walden Pond—more of a lake, really—in a frothing blue below and the sky a bowl of cool, washed light above. Then we walked slowly through a dappled world woven by jeweled leaves and the glimmer of water through bare branches. We were in no hurry. We stopped whenever some thing of beauty caught our eye. We snapped a thousand pictures and talked out all the doubt we had stuffed away during our last busy weeks.

When the brilliance of the leaves was lost in the darkling of dusk, when the lake was a sheet of gold, ringed by brooding trees, we sat for one last minute of hush.

"I feel like I can breathe again," said Joel in the darkness beside me.

I knew exactly what he meant. "I feel like God loves me again," I added, and he nodded agreement.

Through the gift of that day, crammed with loveliness, surrounded by the tangible goodness of God's creation, we once again felt His presence in our lives to be real. The evidence of beauty was so great, we felt strengthened to trust God to help and lead us through all the niggling troubles of our lives.

I think Mary would call that day a star, a point of redemptive light in the midst of a dark time. What does it mean to walk with God in darkness? This is the question I think was at the heart of Joel's doubt and mine, the question I feel Mary had to answer as her heart was pierced again and again with the mysterious "sword" that Simeon foretold.

I have found my walk with God means the endurance of many shadowed days. Not necessarily dark ones of great pain or loss. Dim ones rather, when doubt clouds my view of God in a way that is almost worse than pain because it makes such a miasma of weariness in my soul. Most of life consists of dusty, normal days that are often punctuated by sickness, thorny relationships (especially those involving family), general struggle (a flat tire, money problems, simple irritation), and loneliness. The world is profoundly broken. My own natural impulse in the midst of struggle is to allow discouragement to seep into every vein. I am tempted to a numbness of heart that leaves me incapable of seeing beauty or allowing myself to hope.

But I have come to know that I will never be a strong woman of God unless I understand that such darkness is part of the battle, a part of the burden we bear as humans in a fallen world. What then do I do to keep faith alive and breathing in my tired heart?

I look for beauty. I look for starlight. I have trained myself to seek out and wonder at the goodness of God present even in my dusty days. To seek beauty in the midst of fallenness is to have faith in a reality beyond what I can see. Despite the brokenness of the world around me, my heart still perceives glimmers of what was meant to be, echoes from the shattered beauty of creation. I see hope shining in nature and gleaming from art and music and story. I am aware that there is some force of beauty calling me to look beyond the brokenness and hope for redemption. To walk with God means to fight tooth and nail, day after day, to hold fast to my belief in the happy ending God has promised His children.

I have learned that, sometimes, loving God means crafting a picture of the good I know is coming, the hope I trust will save me, even in the middle of a messy, ordinary day. This takes training. You have to turn away from darkness and force yourself to look upon the beauty of creation, to notice the small gestures of daily affection from your family. Learn how to host a teatime and invite the lonely neighbor when you want to cry. Put on uplifting music when a dirty house must be cleaned. Light a candle and listen to the most beautiful soundtrack you can find instead of sitting alone in your room in despair. Take a day away from it all and breathe and talk and wander until the beauty of God restores your hope.

Mary probably spent the rest of her days after the angel's visit working to believe that the God who started all this drama in her life would see it through to a good end. Her faith would be challenged by the sword of doubt, of fear, of struggle. But I like to believe she had the sort of heart that didn't quail. Oh, I'm sure she cried and ached when loss assailed her. But I think she learned to fight, to rise above the darkness, to lift her face in hope and continue to follow after the God whose grace was evident all around her if only she would take the time to see. I think we can do the same.

When it comes right down to it, everything I believe in lies just beyond my touch. But my love of God drives me to live in a certain way and compels me to picture my hope in my words, my actions, and the set of my face as I encounter the world daily. Though the world is fallen, God's goodness can still be seen there, and the promise of restoration is at the center of my hope. By learning to see His grace, I learn to survive, to be strong, to bear the hurt of living in a fallen world. To look for beauty, to fix your eyes on the starlight, is to live out hope in the perfection of God.

Joel and I took one last walk on our perfect day. Late that night we were back downtown, the buzz of the city loud in our ears again. A full moon hung in the sky, its reflection shimmering on the harbor where we strolled. We knew that the rush of our lives would pick right back up in the morning, but for that instant we were still full of the beauty of our day together. As we talked, we both came to a conclusion.

"It's a battle, isn't it," said Joel, "to keep your heart alive, to keep on hoping? Getting out and looking at beauty, it's like a fight."

"It is," I replied. "Beauty is a battle cry!"

"Yes!" he answered, and we both grinned and knew we were ready to return to the fight.

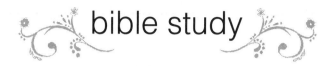

bible study

Psalm 27:4–6

How can you behold the beauty of the Lord today? How is God a refuge for you? Why do you think the psalmist was able to "sing with shouts of joy" even in the presence of his enemies?

Hebrews 12:1–2

Why was Jesus able to endure the shame of the cross? How can you fix your eyes on Jesus in such a way that helps you to walk through a dark time?

Isaiah 40:25–31

What does God say about the stars? How does this ringing affirmation of God's power give you hope? What is promised to those who wait on God and hope in him?

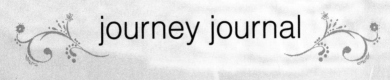

journey journal

chapter six

The Great Adventure

The night lay warm and silky upon them. Joseph turned his head to the tiny window and gazed out at the night sky with its sweep of stars. He lay on his back, helpless to think of what he would tell his wife. Mary was not going to like this. Beside him she slept, her breath steady and sweet. Two more minutes and her heart would quicken with panic when he told her the news. Let her sleep a minute more. He had to gather his courage.

This had been their first home. He had hunted out this tiny house in Bethlehem just after Jesus was born. He picked it for its cozy little room and the tiny garden that would gladden Mary's heart as she regained her strength. Joseph had no trouble finding work; carpenters were always in demand. Mary sang as she cooked and kept house and ran with kisses for Joseph when he came home at night. She made friends quickly and soon knew the markets of Bethlehem as if she had grown up there. Far from gossiping friends, safe from their curiosity, she was free to enjoy the small, sweet rounds of the everyday. They had decided to stay, though for just how long, they felt it unnecessary to decide.

Life these two years had been precious, sweet as a glad dream that comes just before you waken to the rush of day. But waken we all must, and Joseph had felt the nudge of it first when the Magi came. One bright spring day, a caravan of wise men from the royal courts in the East stopped at their simple front door. "Where is the king?" they had asked, breathless with excitement. They claimed they had followed a star to this doorstep, and they had come to worship the new king foretold by prophets. And when they saw the child Jesus, they had fallen to their knees and laid precious gifts at his feet. And Joseph knew, even amidst this wondrous spectacle, that their life was about to change. If these far-flung seers knew of the miraculous child, soon others would as well.

Now Joseph lay awake in the night, wide-eyed with knowledge that the time had come to leave this peaceful existence. He sighed. There was no easy way to do this. He shifted and stroked Mary's arm until she took a sharp, waking breath and opened her eyes.

"Mary?" he said and waited until he knew she would hear him fully. "I've had a dream. An angel came to me."

He heard the quickening of her breath. He couldn't blame her. The visits of angels had never betokened calm.

"What did he say?" Her voice was a whisper in the night.

> "My poor Joseph. You had no idea what you were getting into when you married me."

Joseph felt along the blanket until he found her hand and gripped it hard. He took a deep breath and hesitated.

"Joseph, darling, why won't you answer?" she asked with worried amusement. "I'm starting to get a little afraid of what you might say."

"We must go to Egypt." He spat it out and was done, then lay flat on his back and sighed. The worst was over.

"Egypt? Are you sure?"

"Mary," Joseph sat up now to tell it all, "Herod knows about Jesus. You know the Eastern kings told him of the prophecies. Now Herod wants to destroy him and we have to flee."

There was a moment of silence. "When must we go?"

He coughed, and she nudged him hard in the arm. "Joseph! When?"

"Tonight."

She took it better than he'd thought. She sighed and her breath became steady again. Her hand crept over the blankets and up his shoulder until she found his face in the darkness and patted it like she would a child's.

"My poor Joseph. You had no idea what you were getting into when you married me. Oh, we've been so happy here. I felt safe. I felt almost normal."

They sat a few moments more in the dark, knowing that the instant they left the bed their lives would change once more. So sweet was the silence, the very air seemed to belong to them. But there was a slight shift of black in the sky as dawn sent a flare of warning over the farthest horizon.

Joseph sat up straight.

"We'd better hurry, Mary. Jerusalem is barely a day's march. The soldiers could be here by afternoon."

"I am ready."

With hushed, swift movements, they gathered their belongings. They had added a few things since arriving on the donkey two years before. Mary was determined to pack the few linens and dishes she had scraped together, bits of beauty to brighten whatever new place they were to inhabit. Then there were the gifts of the kings to be carefully wrapped in thick swathes of linen and hidden deep in their packs. The treasure would fund a journey they had not foreseen. When a strip of silvered light blazed on the horizon, Joseph lifted Jesus from his bed and set him on the donkey waiting in the road outside.

He watched as Mary lingered in the doorway and knew that her eyes hungered to impress the small room upon her memory. The house had been her shelter, a place where she had known a few sweet months of rest. Joseph felt the road, pebbled and dusty beneath his feet, like a tumbling river that waited to catch them in its swift flow. Finally, Mary turned, and Joseph saw that her face was settled, her eyes at peace. She stepped into the road and put her hand in his.

"The adventure begins again," she whispered.

Thank goodness she had been ready to go, thought Mary, as the donkey jostled her for a fifth day over the desert. It wasn't as if any woman could ever truly be prepared for a midnight flight into foreign lands, but at least her heart had been right. Poor Joseph, he thought the news would come as a surprise. But when he shook her awake that night, word of his dream was only the end of the long farewell she had already said to the life she loved.

The visit of the Magi had shattered the fancy that her miracle child could stay hidden. Just the hungry wonder in their eyes showed Mary the doggedness with which the world would soon pursue her little boy. The walls of her tiny home could no longer shelter him from restless kings and people in need. From that day forth, Mary had slowly loosened her grip on the life they had built for themselves in Bethlehem.

There was no denying it had been a struggle at first. When Joseph left for his work each day, Mary basked in the peace of her home over and over again. Each bright dish in its place, the flowers in the burnished jug, the table Joseph carved as their first piece of furniture—each of these stabbed at her heart. Why must she leave this life? Why couldn't Jesus grow up in a simple home among loving neighbors? Would they never be allowed to settle down for good? Day by day, a storm gathered in Mary's mind, tightened her face, and hushed her tongue.

Then one morning, Jesus lifted his hands to her with concern etched in every curve of his little round face. "Mommy sad?" he asked. And Mary felt the world about her cease to move, and her own breath halted as she met the troubled gaze of her child. God looked out at her from those eyes, whispered to her in those little boy words. Why was she sad?

Kings had come to her door bearing jewels. Angels sang of the birth, and shepherd's worshiped her baby. Was she not upheld in hands so good and great that their care would never end? Do not be afraid. The words of the angel came to her again. She knew now that he meant much more than for her not to fear in that moment. He may as well have said, "Do not be afraid as you follow God. Do not fear when friends are changeful and your way unexpected. Do not

> **She held her heart out to God and fought to keep her hands open, her fingers loose.**

fear, for you will never be forsaken." Her life had been an uphill clamber since the angel came, yet what prophet or king or any follower of God had known anything different? Jesus' small face was a gentle rebuke. She knelt, the stillness of God's presence before her, sharpening every sense, hushing the air. She lifted Jesus onto her lap and held him close.

"No, Mommy is not sad anymore."

From that moment forward she held her heart out to God and fought to keep her hands open, her fingers loose. She chose which lovely things she would take when the time came to leave and quietly packed food and clothes. And when Joseph whispered in that blackest night, she rose, at rest and ready to go.

Now Mary held Jesus a little more snugly as they rode together on the donkey's back and kissed him as he squirmed his reluctance to sit any longer.

"I know," she whispered in his ear, "I'm tired of riding this donkey too. But just a few more days and we'll be in a big city, and you can laugh and run all you like."

Taking his small, fleshy hand in her own, she tickled and tapped it to distract him while she looked out at the hazy desert landscape. Though no hint of home or human yet colored the ground, she knew that a city lay but a few miles ahead. She smiled in spite of herself. Who would have guessed that little Mary from Nazareth would travel to foreign cities and visit the wide world?

Just two years before, the prospect of such an odyssey would have terrified her to tears. But then, so would have angels and censuses and an audience with exotic kings. Her soul, she felt, had widened, her heart expanded to bear more grief, know more joy. Nothing would make her afraid ever again.

Jesus chuckled and pointed, kicking at the donkey's sides so that the poor beast gave a mournful grunt. Mary looked up and saw Joseph shielding his eyes and peering ahead. The sun was finally in its swoon in the western sky, and Mary saw a bump on the far horizon. City gates! They would reach the great place by nightfall.

Joseph turned. "Well, we're almost there. Are you all right, Mary?

She smiled, hugged her boisterous child, and took a deep breath of dry desert air.

"Yes," she beamed, "I am."

A dance, that's what the city was, a wild, never-ending whirl of faces and colors and sounds. In those first days in Egypt, Mary walked the streets like a woman in a dream, eyes bedazzled by the teeming crowds, heart startled by the scents and songs she had never known existed.

For a time, they sojourned in the Jewish section and found neighbors swift in their kindness. In a foreign land where all strangers were far from home, friendships formed quickly. Joseph found work, while Mary made do in a small house shared with another family. Jesus whooped his joy in the multitude of playmates. Mary's new friends showed her the rounds of water and washing and work. Best of all, they took her to the markets where merchants from every civilized country hawked their wares.

Mary felt she had stumbled headlong into a fantastical myth where people from every corner of the world gathered to talk and sell and argue the day away. She fingered the dusky purple of a vendor's Phoenician cloth. She touched intricate boxes carved in the farthest East and saw gold hammered thin and woven into jewelry that stole her breath away. The people from a hundred lands brushed against her as she walked, each bearing a faith and story of their own.

When she walked through the marketplace hand in hand with Jesus, she knew she held the desire of all peoples, the secret treasure of the universe. She would glance down at her son, then back up at the roiling mix of cultures. And she knew it was her son for whom all peoples of the earth hoped, even if they did not yet know it.

Indeed, the city was a cry for peace and provision. The fierce lament of the needy tore at her heart with a dirge that thrummed beneath the colors and smiles. She saw as never before the wretches who hovered in dirty corners, begging for bread. She saw the painted women who lounged in dark corners, bereft of laughter or life. She saw slaves weep and soldiers bellow and children die from hunger and sickness.

Yet she also rejoiced at the wild path on which God led her, this unknown way in which she saw the needs of the world writ large in the city, told small in the lives of all she passed. Here she heard the cry of the whole earth yearning for God. She saw the great, aching, beloved wreck of a world and people broken by sin. And when she looked at Jesus, she felt ablaze with the wonder of his presence, the fathomless truth of God come down among men.

And she taught him to see. As Jesus grew, she took him often into the streets, showing him beggars and hollow-cheeked children, kneeling with him to give them a bit of food. She took him to city heights to hear trumpets sounding and voices raised in song, to see the smoke rising from the hearths of a thousand homes as the great sun set. She told him the stories of prophets and kings and whispered that he would be greater than them all, mighty in love and in laughter, and bring life to the dying earth.

When the angel came next, Mary knew it by the way Joseph tossed beside her. Like water, dawn filled their small room with crystalline light that climbed the walls and flooded their eyes. Mary lay wakeful, waiting to hear the news of Joseph's dream. She felt his eyes open, felt the calm loveliness of the morning pool around them. Finally, she could stand it no longer. She turned, eyes wide and bright.

"You had a dream?"

"Why yes," he breathed, sitting up. "Mary, we can go home."

"I know," she whispered and lay back as a strange feeling rose in her throat, the sweetness of hope with the bitter taste of an ending. "I can barely believe it. I used to yearn for this day."

"Do you not now?" he asked, startled.

"Oh, yes." She smiled, turning her face so that he could see the joy she felt. "Yet I am sad to leave. Joseph, we have seen so much. I am so different now. I see . . . ," she struggled to voice her thought. "I see how much the world needs our little boy. And how sweet a gift he is. And I'm sorry to leave it, that's all."

He nodded, and they both lay back to bask in the quiet. Once again, when they stepped out it would be on a new path running swiftly beneath their feet. A rueful light came to Mary's eyes. The endings weren't getting any easier, but hope grew. Faith blossomed. The road led on, and she would follow it.

"I'm ready," she breathed and put her feet on the floor.

devotional

My mother calls it "crossing the bridge."

She did it herself when she was twenty-four, just out of college, and fired up with the love of God. At a student conference, she heard a missionary issue a passionate challenge to young Christians to move to communist Poland to bring life and help to a discouraged people. "Yes!" cried my mother in her heart, sure that every other person there felt the same. But out of hundreds of people, only she and three others responded. When I ask her why, she replies with that phrase and a shrug of her shoulders. "Well, I was crossing the bridge from normal life to kingdom life. I told God I would go anywhere and do anything. I knew my life would probably be an unexpected adventure from there on out, but I was ready."

So off to Poland she went. The next three years were made up of secret meetings, bananas purchased on the black market, and covert Bible studies with young Polish students. Her faith was tempered like steel, her love refined like gold, and it all began because she crossed the bridge she calls "the willingness to go anywhere."

Mary crossed the same bridge. Think of what her life must have been like after she said yes to the angel Gabriel. Not only was she subject to suspicion from her neighbors and the persecution of kings, but she was forced to move and travel more than any village girl of the time would ever have expected. Whisked to Bethlehem, chased to Egypt, then returning to her hometown of Nazareth, Mary's life as God's chosen was that of a nomad. She and Joseph had no plan, no promise of comfort. Yet a more faithful, surer heart was never found, for she followed and "pondered" and set out once again whenever God beckoned.

Mary gives us a model I have followed closely in recent years because I find that my own faith constantly demands more of me than I ever expected. When I first began to follow Jesus, I assumed that a godly life meant walking a gentle upward road of righteousness. I assumed that I would become increasingly perfect, perhaps even more beautiful as the virtuous heroines in old tales always do. If my upward road required climbing the occasional hill of suffering or challenge of ministry or work, I thought it would be a momentary trial I would climb with admirable grace, emerging on the other side with increased wisdom and a new appreciation for the beauty of sunshine and flowers. Every day I would advance another mile of goodness until by, say, twenty-five, I would have this "holiness" thing down pat. And, of course, I would be very happy, because we all know virtue ought to fill one with deep and lasting joy.

Reality has confounded me.

Life has commandeered my days with all the grace of an invading army, crushing my expectations and saddling me with loneliness and health problems and impossible writing projects instead. It never occurred to me that God would allow sickness or loneliness in my life. I certainly never expected to struggle to figure out His presence or purpose as I shaped my plans and goals. I thought these things would be settled once I became an adult Christian, and yet I have sometimes raged in confusion at it all.

The past year has been one of my hardest. God and I have grappled like Jacob and the angel in the desert. I was determined to have a life plan written in stone, and He was just as certain that I needed to wait. *Give me friends,* I raged. *Give me stability and a definite plan for my future!* He didn't. At my wit's end one day, I blurted out, "I feel like the most unstable person in the world!"

I said this to my dear friend Jossie. She is one of the warmest, dearest people I have ever met. Since I have known her, she has lost her baby girl, gone through major changes, and worked to raise four adorable, rambunctious little boys. Never have I met a woman with a heart so set on faithful loving God. We were at her house when I voiced my own frustration. She looked at me with the kind of understanding that makes you feel known right down to your toes.

"Oh, Sarah, you're not unstable. Your life just isn't sure right now. But God is stable. And you know, He's taken our hands off the steering wheel. God is taking my pain and asking me to trust Him. He's taking your life and asking you to do the same. He wants us to trust Him, not ourselves."

She reached over and placed a tiny teacup ornament in front of me. The plate beneath it had broken, but the tiny chintz cup was still whole. I laughed because I knew this cup—it was a gift to Jossie from my mom. My mom had given it to a few friends to symbolize the cup that God gives each of us to drink. "Drink it with grace," my mom would say.

Jossie laughed as I held the cup. "Look at that," she said. "The plate just shattered the other day when I dropped it, but the cup is still intact. That's exactly how I feel about my life. God is letting the foundations I thought I needed fall away, but His goodness remains the same. The cup is still intact. I struggle so much with changes and pain in my life, but God is teaching me that all I need to do is hold tight to Him. Not my expectations or my anger or my weakness. Just Him. And He keeps me safe through it all."

Jossie knew a secret that all lovers of God must learn.

Loving God means to join the battle, to fight evil, to struggle with suffering and sin. Loving God means giving the lives we thought we could control into the hands of a wild and loving Father who takes us where we need to go, not where we want.

Following God doesn't mean having a normal, scheduled, painless life. If you and I are going to be God's own women and follow Him to the ends of the earth, we have to cross that bridge of willingness and face the wild future as it comes. Loving God means bringing His beauty to the darkest of places. It means receiving unexpected visits from needy people, picking up and moving to Poland (or Egypt) when you're not ready, and undertaking inconvenient adventures.

If we trust God to lead us in His own beautiful path, if we remove our white-knuckled fingers from the wheel, He will take us just where we need to go and make us all that we need to be. To truly belong to Him, we must lay down every expectation except the sure knowledge that He will uphold us. And when you are cradled in the palms of love itself, you don't have to be afraid.

To become a woman like Mary, you must hold life loosely in your open hands, ready to yield to God and receive whatever He gives. Yes, life will be an adventure, a quest, a challenge. Your days will burn bright with miracles and blaze with beauty. And yes, darkness will dog you, and doubt will be a mist in your eyes. But this is the way of it with those who love God with all their heart, mind, soul, and strength. Amy Carmichael and C. S. Lewis, Jim Elliot and George Mueller, they knew this. Every hero in the Bible and every experienced servant of God knows that to follow Christ you must cross that bridge in your heart and say, "Lord, bring it."

Let the adventure begin.

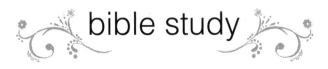

bible study

Philippians 3:7–14

Do you consider Jesus and His kingdom worth giving your whole life for? How can you "press on" toward the goal of Christ? What things have you had to count as loss in your own life with God? Has it been worth it?

Hebrews 11:13–16

Why were the men and women in this passage able to endure? What was their hope? What country were they headed for?

Genesis 12:1–3

What would have happened if Abraham had refused to "go forth to the land God showed him"? Isn't it interesting that the history of God's people began with a wanderer. Are you willing to go forth if God calls you?

journey journal

part three

Esther

chapter seven

Heart Alive

She felt damp, like a soaked piece of girlhood moldering away in a gloomy palace, instead of the prospective queen she was. The stone-walled rooms of the palace felt ever wet from the daily baths she had to endure. Esther was just one among many lovely women, all being prettied and pampered into prospective wives for the great, and rather petulant, king. Their keepers told them this year of cosmetic treatments was necessary to cultivate their beauty to its highest form. The keepers did not add that the king would pick his pleasure from among them. He would choose his favorite like a lazy boy sorting good apples until he has found the shiniest one. Then he would carelessly toss the rest away into his harem, their luster and lives bruised by his touch.

Esther felt that her skin would soon dissolve in the daily salt scrubbings and perfumed soakings that set the cadence of her days. These treatments supposedly cleansed their victims of blemish by sloughing all roughness and stain away. What they really cleansed, thought Esther, was any sense of self. Luxury made all the girls alike. The attendants painted their eyes and perfumed their hair, dressing them in robes unbearably lovely yet the same until every spark of individuality and spirit fizzled out of their eyes. Forget your past life, they were told every day. Leave behind the blemished girl you once were. And with it, thought Esther, your soul.

Esther's fist came down hard against the window ledge. She must not give in. As moonlight illuminated her eyes with an icy flame, she took a deep breath, determined to keep her heart alive.

It was easier at first, when the fire of courage quickened her heart. When the soldiers stomped to her door, armed against all resistance, she stepped out with head held high, shoulders thrown back in a grace that defied her captors. She felt like a martyr, a soul determined not to yield even in the hands of her enemies. Her first days in the palace were marked by the will to be brave. She met each new woman with bright eyes and a sisterly embrace, intent upon building friendships in this cushioned cage. But the valor that pulsed in her veins died down as the days stretched into weeks, then months, in which her old life was ruthlessly washed away. Her steps were contained to garden paths, her every move watched by implacable soldiers. This life of baths, gardens, and soulless beauty bore in upon her heart until she could no longer escape the reality of her situation and gave in to tears.

Her old life was gone. Never again would she sit by the fire and whisper with her uncle Mordecai, who had raised her as his own. Never again would she sing with her people, or hear the words of her God read on Sabbath days. Never again would she tumble in play with the children of her village, eavesdrop on the matchmaking old women, or join the feasts that marked life as worthy of celebration. All had been irrevocably lost to the whim of a selfish king.

She was glad to cry then, for her pain formed within her a heartbroken resolve. Mourning let her keep hold of all that was lost. To grieve was to clutch her memories like jewels, to finger these precious things and resist the forces that would cleanse her of her past.

But then even grief died away. One young girl can scarcely sustain a soldier's courage or a mourner's passionate pain for more than a few weeks. When one of the stewards sat her down for a stern lecture regarding her tears, she was too tired to resist. They said that tears only spoiled her face and darkened the spirits of all around her, and soon, for the sake of peace, she agreed.

And then she felt nothing at all. She bathed and ate, sang and smiled, turned on cue for weeks on end, and bore it all in silence. No longer did she offer herself in friendship or let an unguarded word fall from her tongue. Her spirit retreated into a high-walled room of lost hope, and silence became a shield that protected her heart from her captors. She maintained her grace, kept the habit of kindness that Mordecai had woven so deeply into her. But her spirit withdrew from her eyes, the warmth faded from her face, and she no longer ventured forth from the dark, sad confines of her thoughts.

Then one day, when she found herself nodding in mechanical agreement to a maid's haughty slur of "filthy Jews," Esther sat straight up as she became aware of the words. The name of her own people, spoken in this foreign place, ripped through the quiet and tore apart her calm. Her face turned crimson with guilt that such a thing should be spoken and she not refute it. Eyes burning, she looked at the circle of women about her, each of whose face was either vacant or vaguely sad. None protested the maid's cruel words.

Esther sat straighter, determined to speak out. She could not openly declare herself a Jewess—Mordecai's last charge had been that she guard this secret with her life. But now, heady with anger, her temples throbbing with emotion and the strong perfumes, Esther leaned forward to speak in garbled protest. Shocked, the maid glanced up, her eyebrows arched in irritation.

> **She must find a way to live, to fight.**

"What?" she rasped and did not wait for a reply. "Back to the baths with you," she barked at Esther, "you're looking pale."

And Esther stood, for her body had been trained to automatic obedience. But the quiet of her soul had been shattered. Panic knocked down the door to her heart, and she realized she had been like a dead woman. She had pushed away the memory of those she loved, the God she served, and had dwelt in blackness. Now she knew she must not fade into silence. She must find a way to live, to fight, even though she had not chosen this life and did not want it.

That night, when the liquid black of the small hours kept the watchful maids at bay, she rose. She crept to the stone sill of her window and knelt there. And she began to restore her soul to life.

Her first duty was to accept the fact of her changed life, to settle her mind firmly on the truth of her palace existence. To love, to laugh in this place had seemed a betrayal of all she had lost, so she had refused all happiness, as if she could keep hold of the old life by refusing to love the new. Now she looked her loss full in the face and knew the past was out of reach. She opened her hand and let go of the life she once loved.

She had thought she would feel utterly bereft, but as she sat in the darkness, there came a sudden comfort. The memories settled around her, not as torture, but as grace. The faces of her friends, the old habit of laughter, the little delights of daily life came to her as solace. Her former life, she saw, had been a gift, for there had been many friendships made, meals tasted, and songs sung. To forget would be to betray these gifts of her past. Instead, she knew she must carry it with her, to bring the joy had known into this gloomy palace, to offer life to the lonely souls it sheltered.

She sat a little straighter in the moonlight.

Yes, she must drag life with her into this forsaken place.

Esther yawned. That was all the vim she had for this night. But the veil of grief that had covered her was gone, and when she woke come the dawn, a new light glimmered in her heart as well—hope.

She was timid at first, determined but shy in her effort to know the people near her. One morning she whispered a question to the woman who sat beside her during a beauty treatment. With hunger in her eyes, the girl replied, and Esther soon heard the tale of her life before the palace. From that moment, they were fast friends.

Such small steps, timid reaches into the dark, soon brought her joy and laughter, the first she had tasted since leaving her home. And day by day, the light came back to her eyes.

And as it did, the hushed, sweet voice of her God returned to grace her thoughts. *Trust me*, he said. *Love me.* She stiffened at first, for he had not kept her from this place, had not staid the soldier's hands or hidden her from their eyes, and the future yawned before her uncertain. But as friendship gathered about her, and strength returned to her spirit, she yielded and lifted her eyes up at night. And she learned to pray again. God was the beautiful King who made her people what they were. He was true even when she was in exile, and somehow, he was with her in this place.

So peace came back to Esther, flushed her face and gentled her speech, and those who watched her felt wonder rise up like a hunger in their souls. The other women drew near her, and even the head steward, Hegai, watched her closely, drawn to her joyful presence.

One hot, bright morning, Esther woke to the insistent call of the attendants. All the candidates were to assemble in the long, ivied passageway that led to the garden. Esther followed the others outdoors where the warm air was fresh and scented by the garden. The women nudged each other and whispered in curiosity. But when Hegai stood to address the women, Esther listened closely. Change was in the air.

"It is time," rumbled the steward Hegai, clearing his throat, "for each of you to have a personal maid. These girls have been selected to serve you as you enter the final months of your preparation for the king. They are trained in all the arts of beauty, but unlike the women who have attended you thus far, the girl assigned to you shall be your personal maid alone. A gift from the king."

And with that, a line of young girls filed in from the garden to face the waiting women. Robed in identical white dresses, each with a flower in her braided hair, some

> **A good heart had brought her the gift of this child.**

had square faces and others round. Some mouths were dimpled by habitual laughter, some pensive and pursed. Their eyes were hued in all the varied browns of the rich earth. As Hegai led each child to her new mistress, Esther spotted one that held her glance. She was a small girl, sturdy in body, yet with an elusive frailty in the way she lifted her face in delicate hope. Each time Hegai came to take another child's hand, Esther watched the child's eyes lift, eyebrows poised in expectation, then fall when she was passed by. When Hegai finally brought her out from the line, she clung to his hand with the trusting grasp of a daughter. He led her straight to Esther.

"Her name is Naia," he said, placing the small hand in Esther's own. "I saw," he hesitated and lowered his eyes, "a gentleness in her. The same as I see in you."

An ache rose in Esther's throat. Hegai would say no more, but she knew now that a kind eye had been watching her, a good heart had brought her the gift of this little child.

Esther knelt and looked her little maid in the face. At first, Naia dropped her eyes and kept her head obediently down. Submission masked her features, and Esther hurt to know that at court even little girls must keep the tumult of their thoughts from their faces. She wondered what fate had severed this child from her family and set her in the palace. Esther spoke her name and put a gentle hand on her shoulder. Naia raised the black flash of her eyes to Esther's face.

"I'm glad you are here," said Esther. "I've wanted a friend."

For a moment the mask slipped and hope blazed on Naia's cheeks before she dropped her eyes and stood docile again.

But Esther gripped her hand all the tighter. She would bring joy back to those eyes and liven this little face with laughter. She stood. "Come Naia," she said, and took the child's arm in the same protective way that Mordecai had taken hers when they strolled the marketplace in the old, happy days. "I'll show you our room."

At first, Naia served with a quiet perfection, scampering from task to task like a little mouse, intent upon her work, determined not to fail. To Esther's questions or even laughter, she responded with prim reserve. The mask did not slip again from her eyes, and Esther began to wonder if she could ever reach her little maid's heart.

Then one late night, as Esther sat by her window, she heard a cry like the sob of a baby. Near, yet deeply muffled. She slipped into the hall and followed the cries until they led her to the maids' room at the end of the corridor. Esther knew it was her girl who wept in the blackness. She whispered Naia's name and called her to come.

Naia obediently tiptoed through the maze of beds and sleeping girls, her eyes wide with fear. Finger to her lips, Esther led Naia back to her room, and there she drew the little girl close. Finally, the mask slipped and Naia wept openly. And then she talked. She told Esther of the family she had lost and whispered her fear of the darkness to her mistress. When dawn crept in through the window, Naia's face was curved happily with hope.

From then Naia was a maid in name only. To Esther, she was a friend and daughter. Naia plied her arts in beauty full well, priding herself on perfecting the charms of her mistress. Among all the women in the palace, none was better coiffed or clothed than Esther. Naia bustled about the palace rooms with her face in a gladsome tilt. But when the doors were shut at night and the other maids were asleep, Naia nestled into the crook of Esther's arm as she once had in her mother's and listened to Esther tell stories and sing songs to chase her fears away. Esther sheltered the child, making her world small and safe again. Day by day Esther grew to love the child, and love grew in the child's face.

And night after night, Esther prayed. The day of the king's choice was drawing near. Soon, Esther knew, her life would change again. Just how, she did not yet know. But just when she had thought she could no longer endure, joy had come to her again. Now she must cling with all her might to hope, and trust that joy would follow her beyond the next stage of her palace life.

When the day arrived, Naia was more aflutter with worry than Esther. She fussed like an old woman, making certain that every flower be fixed just right in Esther's dark hair, and that the folds of her white dress fall in the most winsome way.

Hegai stopped in to check on the preparations and looked on the two girls with something near to a fatherly gleam. Esther smiled, thanking him for the gift he had brought her in Naia. When it was time to select her jewelry, she asked his advice.

"Go simply as you are," he said, to her surprise. "The light of your face is enough. And Naia has made everything else just as it should be. I wish you well, Esther."

Esther rose, her face flushed. She turned, and with a last pat of Naia's head and a last nod to Hegai, she walked out the door. For the first time in a year, she was escorted into the wider maze of the palace.

The king's breath caught in his throat.

In slow, steady grace, the woman walked down the hall to kneel at the foot of his throne. Already she held his heart. Of all the women Hegai had marched before him, only this one required nothing more to make her a queen. Royalty flowed from every aspect of her being. Dignity was apparent in the high tilt of her head, grace in the flow of her step. And her bright, knowing eyes were regal in their quiet, as if she held a secret joy. Radiant she was, as if the air danced about her. Love shone from her eyes, and kindness formed the contours of her face. This was a woman to turn the soul of a king.

He held out his scepter.

Queen she would be in name as she already was in heart.

"Look at me Esther," he said.

It was the gentlest of commands.

devotional

I was twenty-one when I got my first real job, and it was a good one—administrative work in an office near my house, weekends off, and great pay. I felt like an adult. I had money, I had a car, I was independent. And I was miserable. The 9-to-5 routine did not in any way fit my ideals or my dreams. At the beginning of that year, I wrote out my goals for the coming months. I wanted to write, to travel, to live outside the box, meet new people, discover new cultures, and pretty much be a wild-eyed dreamer.

But then real life barged in, demanding that I earn money and take responsibility for my commitments and expenses. Before I knew it, I was tied to a job requiring intensive detail work that drained my creativity and left me too worn out to meet my writing goals. In no way did sitting in an office in my hometown five days a week, answering emails and organizing bank deposits, fulfill my hopes and desires.

I turned silent and stoic in my frustration. I showed up at the office each day, worked hard and well, and then went home to stew. Though I spent the better part of my week at work, I didn't invest any of my self or soul into my life there. I brought nothing personal to decorate my workspace, ate granola bars for lunch, and looked forward to the weekends. I thought maybe I could stave off the reality of my situation by refusing to become invested in this life I did not want.

My dawn walks up a mountain trail near my house were my only outlet for wrestling the emotions that raged inside. One blindingly sunny morning, as I struggled up the steepest part of the trail, I became so frustrated and out of breath, I finally told God exactly what I thought. I stopped, bent double from lack of air at high altitude, sucked a bit of oxygen into my lungs, and turned my face to the sky. "God," I said with unbridled annoyance, "I know you're probably disappointed in me. But honestly, I feel disappointed with you."

With my frustration spoken, the spunk went out of me and I sat down on a rock at the top of the trail. Why had God done this to me when all I wanted to do was love Him with a wild, free heart? This was not the life I had expected or wanted. God knew my spirit, He knew my creative bent, and He knew my hatred of schedules and details. Yet here He had plunked me into a desk job when I had trusted Him to do something wondrous and new with me.

I put my head in my hands and whispered my prayer aloud. The nice thing about mountain trails is you can talk openly with only the trees and sky to overhear. "Lord," I blubbered, "I can't move past irritation or exhaustion. I can't accept this life as enough to fill the desires of my heart. I have no peace, and part of me doesn't want to. I don't want to accept that this is where you want me."

But as I expressed my anger, the bitterness seeped out with my words, and suddenly I felt tearful as a little girl. "God," I whispered, "I just wanted to know you. I wanted to go into missions or be a St. Teresa and spend hours in prayer and make beautiful things. And now, I'm not even sure you *like* me any more. But I can't just sit in my apartment and work at my desk and feel that it's enough. I want to know you, but I don't know how to do it in the life I have."

My real grievance was confusion and the way it put God far from me. I couldn't accept God's will, and so I felt lost as a child in a dark, fairy-tale forest. With this realization like a stone in my heart, I shuffled down the mountainside and drove back home. In a huff of heart-sickness, with confusion shrouding my heart like a mountain mist, I plopped into my red wingback chair and opened my Bible. *At least I was still having quiet times*, I thought with a doleful glance at the page.

But the first words I saw clutched at my heart:

I sought him whom my soul loves,
I sought him but did not find him.
I must arise now and go about the city;
In the streets and in the squares
I must seek him whom my soul loves.
(Song of Solomon 3:1–2, NASB)

If a voice had spoken these words out of the blue, I couldn't have been more startled. It was as if God reached out from the page and told me He knew my struggle, my need, my yearning for Him. But, came His challenge, would I arise and search for "Him whom my soul loves"?

In that instant, I saw the coward I had been. Like a soldier who slinks away in the shadows from a fight he wants no part of, I had avoided facing my life. I so despised my circumstances that I had not even engaged with them. I wasn't really living my life; I was tolerating time until it passed me by.

I wasn't even seeking God. Instead, I was hiding like Adam after he sinned and God called to him in the garden. I was huddled in a corner, avoiding God's face. I was furious with God, yet terrified of Him. I felt red-cheeked in heart with the shame of it. Right then, in my red chair, with me due at the office any moment, I told God I would get back up and run after Him again, even in this life I so despised.

Sometimes, loving God looks very different from what you think it will. Sometimes God asks you to live a life, or even a phase of life, that feels like the opposite of everything you hoped or wanted. Sometimes there are people so difficult to relate to you think God is punishing you, or a job so ill-suited to your passion that you feel persecuted just to do it.

Yet God knows the plans He has for us. God knows when a young girl is in training to be a queen, or a teenage shepherd is on his way to ruling a kingdom. When faced with a desert time you don't understand, you have a momentous decision ahead of you. You can do as I did at first and hunch down in a despairing little heap and refuse to look life in the face. Or you can do what I think Esther (and so many others in the Bible did) and face your new circumstances with a fight.

One of the traits I see in every biblical hero and heroine is the will to overcome. The men and women God chose are the ones who would step up to fight. Sometimes it was messy and painful, as when Jacob wrestled God in the desert. Sometimes it was valiant, as when David slew Goliath. Sometimes it took a mighty vow like Ruth's, or a heartfelt plea like Hannah's. But God will always engage the hearts of those who choose to wrestle with faith instead of abandoning it. He rejoices in those who would rather fight with God Himself than leave His love behind.

Esther was a young girl separated from her family, taken from the arms of her people, and placed in a foreign court, surrounded idols and pagan gods and who knows what. It's remarkable that she remained loyal to God. We know from the latter portions of her story that Esther kept her Jewish identity alive in her heart. Her belief in God was so strong, she was willing to die for it.

The only way she could have maintained such faith in this foreign land was if she fought for it every day. I think she must have whispered God's words to herself, wrestled with doubt, and fought until she couldn't *not* believe in God's plan. We know from Scripture that Esther found favor in the eyes of her keepers, so she must have kept a kind and tender heart. She had lost everything from her old life, but instead of shriveling up in a ball, she made the choice to live, to love, and to seek and obey the will of her Lord.

And eventually, so did I. I pushed back my pride and discontent and decided that I would make my little office lovely. I brought pictures from home and purchased fresh flowers for my desk. I packed meals that I might actually enjoy and ate them in the common room with my coworkers. I played music. I battled boredom with books during the long afternoon hours, and I fought every hint of despair as it presented itself.

A small fight, yes, but one that strengthened me for the larger fights I will meet in my journey of faith. A fight, I hope, that makes me more like an Esther or Daniel or David in the eyes of God. I want to be a woman who's willing to jump right into the fray for any fight God might ask of me. I want to be like Esther, and I have realized that hers was a fighting, singing, stare-down-the-storm kind of spirit. This is the kind of heart I strive to cultivate every day. Maybe I'll end up a queen after all.

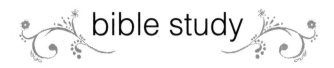 bible study

Romans 12:9–12

What kind of person does this passage describe? What does it mean to "keep your spiritual fervor"? How can you awaken this fervor in your own heart, even when you are discouraged?

1 John 5:3–5

How are we able to "overcome the world"? What might "the world" be in your life, the things that hurt or disappoint you and keep you from engaging your faith? Who truly overcomes the world? And how can you follow Him?

Romans 12:21

This verse is often applied to relationships, but how can you apply it to your circumstances as well? What is an "evil," or irritating, circumstance in your life? How can you overcome it with good?

Revelation 2:6–7

Why do you think God values overcomers so highly? What do you think it takes to be an overcomer? What is it that you need to overcome?

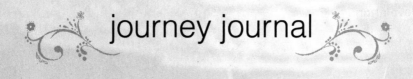

journey journal

chapter eight

For Such a Time

Naia's eyes sprang open at the first hint of sun. Slipping quickly from her bed, she pulled the gauzy curtains back from the window and let the early morning spill in. A chorus of groans assailed her from behind, but she paid no mind. Naia was now first maid in service to the queen, and she saw her position as sacred. Queen Esther must be served as no other queen in Persia ever had been, and Naia kept all the maids in a merry dance of duty each day.

"Up, up, up!" she cried, with a matronly tap of her fingers on the head of the nearest girl. "We have much to do, and Queen Esther will be waiting."

Naia lingered to see that all the girls tumbled out of bed and were well on their way to the tasks assigned them before she slipped, swift and glad, out the door and into the garden. Here she was all girl, lithe and joyous, the firm stance of authority giving way to a childlike patter as she ran.

In a far, fragrant corner, among the flowers, Esther sat in quiet. To Naia, Esther was mother and queen, friend and goddess. Esther's kindness was steadfast, her patience unchanging. But it was her beauty, her quick laughter, and the way she pulled Naia close to her heart that bound the servant girl's love to her for life. If ever the queen should die, Naia thought she would too.

Esther's back was turned so she did not see her maid's approach. The queen's hair was loose over the flowing white robe that Naia placed beside her bed each night. At dawn, Esther always crept out to her garden seat, careful not to wake her maids, knowing that Naia would fetch her when all was ready for the day. Naia walked softly now, an impish smile at the corners of her mouth as she poised herself to startle the queen. But as Esther's face came into view, she stopped.

The queen's eyes were closed, her hands held palms up and out, her face lifted to the dawn light. "Hear O Israel, the Lord is One . . ."

Naia heard the whispered words of her queen, and she froze.

Esther spoke the prayer of a Jew. Only the people of Israel, a small, captive nation, believed there was only one God. Naia had heard her father scoff at this belief countless times. "Why worship one god when there were so many to choose from?" he would say, laughing. Naia's eyes grew wide with the shock of realization that her queen was a Jewess. How could she not have seen it before? The way Esther avoided the idols and kept to her chambers on festival days. The food she would not touch, the sacrifices she would not watch. The prayers she sang to her maids when they were fearful. The psalms she whispered at bedtime each night.

Naia could not move. She didn't felt wonder or anger or even curiosity. She felt only fear as it prickled up her arms and rattled in her heart. Her love for Esther made Naia's eyes and ears sharp to any who would threaten her queen. It was common knowledge that Haman, close counselor to the king, hated the Jews. Therefore, no one must be allowed to know that the queen was a Jewess. Naia herself must not even seem to know.

Esther heard the rustle of her maid's step and turned, her face alight with welcome.

"Good morning, Naia!"

Her voice was a vibrant contrast to the fear that rooted Naia to the ground.

> "Oh, my queen, you must not ever tell!"

"You're so pale, Naia. Come here. What's wrong?"

There was no hiding her shock from the queen, and Naia sat beside her, tongue in a knot. Esther's eyes were two hot lights upon her, searching her face until Naia suddenly blurted, "Oh, my queen, you must not ever tell! You must not let anyone else see that you are one of the Hebrews!"

Esther tilted her head back at that, comprehension quieting her features. She folded her hands in her lap and looked at her maid with gentle concern.

"You heard me praying."

Naia nodded.

Esther put her hand over Naia's small, trembling one. "Naia, I'm so glad. I can't tell you how long I have wanted to share this with you, this God I worship, the faith of my people. This is the heart of who I am, but I have not been able to tell you because my uncle told me to keep it a secret at court."

"And he was right!" The words escaped Naia before she could help it. Emboldened, she continued. "My lady, Haman is in great power at court, and he hates the Jews. You must not tell anyone else."

"For now," she agreed, "I won't. But I will talk about it with you, if you will let me. I have yearned to tell you, my dearest friend. All those songs I sing to you at night . . . You could pray with me if you wanted."

Naia stiffened at the mere thought. She couldn't help it. She had no desire to know this one God, especially when he endangered all she loved. Gods aplenty filled the land. She lowered her eyes, and for the first time since those early days with Esther, she could not look her mistress in the face. Naia did not want a new god. She wanted only to be left in peace. She stood and backed away, head tilted down.

"I must go and see that breakfast is ready."

Esther's hand went to her heart. Dear little Naia, afraid of the whole world, now hurt by the one woman who loved her so well. Hurt by the love Esther bore for God. Sitting on her garden bench, Esther bit her lip and thought there were probably a thousand ways she could have said it better. She ached now to explain, to win Naia's heart, to protect her from anger and fear. But the child had fled.

Esther stood, a sigh in her throat, and walked back to her rooms. She did not fear for herself, but the secret was a hard one to keep. It was true, she had longed for many weeks to tell Naia of the true God she worshiped. But Mordecai's caution had sealed her lips.

As the hum of her maids' voices reached her in the garden, Esther quickened her step, remembering that breakfast was early today, for this was the morning when "the tall man" came. At the thought of this name her maids had given her visitor, Esther lifted her head and felt lighter. Today she would see Mordecai, and never had she known a trouble he could not help.

Since being crowned queen, Esther felt that her life was a series of miracles, one of the best being that Mordecai, her uncle and adopted father, could now visit her. He was a man of no small standing, and now his niece was queen. Esther counted on his visits as if they were food for her heart every bit as vital as sustenance for her body.

When she entered her rooms, each maid glanced up with a small bow and hurried to finish the setting of the queen's table. Bowls of fruits and jugs of fresh juice were set out on a richly woven cloth. Naia was in her usual place beside Esther's chair, ready to fill her plate and cup and fetch any luxury the queen might require. But her head was down, her eyes averted so that Esther could not catch her glance.

Esther ate quickly then ordered the fruit to be left for her visitor. The maids dispersed to do other chores, while Naia and a few others straightened the room and set everything in readiness for the tall man. Esther sat at the table, knowing her uncle would come blustering in, lean and affectionate, at any minute.

An hour passed, and Esther grew restless. She found a seat near the window and gazed across the courtyard to the palace gates, scanning the space for Mordecai's tall, spare form. A business affair, perhaps, had kept him from the palace. Another hour passed, and the usual time of his visit had come and gone. The sun rose high in the sky, and worry crept into Esther's heart. This was not like her uncle.

By the time the midday meal was served, Esther had become truly concerned. Naia's fears were not unjustified, and Esther knew that the climate under Haman's rule was a dangerous one for Mordecai and her people. Esther shook her head as she could only sit and wait. How that hateful man had become second in power to the king was a mystery to her. Haman terrified Esther, though she would never admit it to Naia.

She had first seen the man at a feast given in honor of his new position. He had bowed before her, his eyes darting to her face as he stood. She glimpsed in his eyes a hunger, not clean and honest but grasping and cruel, a need for power that burned in his soul. His words were smooth on surface and spiked within. He bowed in obeisance but stood high and haughty in his heart. She had already seen this played out in the way he ruthlessly destroyed his enemies and grabbed at every honor he could. Esther knew that Mordecai was among the few who refused to acknowledge Haman's ridiculous command that all bow before him as though he were king. Had Haman taken offense and arrested her uncle?

The afternoon came, heavy with heat and a languorous calm. Esther sent her maids to rest, needing solitude in which to still her heart. But Naia asked to stay. The two of them sat, sipping juice from tall, cool glasses, an awkward silence between them. Every now and then, Naia would bite her lip, and Esther sensed that she wanted to say more of their talk from that morning. But just as Naia finally turned full round to face Esther, her eyes moist with entreaty, a knock fell heavily on Esther's door.

Naia opened it to Hathach, the advisor chosen by the king to serve his queen in matters of state. Esther stood, for the advisor's face was troubled. He frowned as he bowed to his queen.

"Mordecai?" Esther asked.

"Yes, my queen. He is not hurt, but he is at the gate in sackcloth and ashes."

"Hathach, run to him now and find out what is the matter. Sackcloth and ashes means death. I must know why he is in mourning. "

When Hathach returned from his errand, he was pale, his face lined with dread. He shook like a small child as he bowed again and gave her the news that the Jews were to be destroyed, every man, woman, and child. On a certain day and month, they were all to be slaughtered and their lands and houses plundered. And all by proclamation of the king, written in every language of Persia and sent to the farthest corners of the empire. But Esther knew who was the author of the order: Haman. Hater of all who opposed him, he was the mortal enemy of Mordecai, and this was his revenge.

> **She glimpsed in Haman's eyes a hunger, a need for power that burned in his soul.**

"May God help us," whispered Esther, then gasped and put her hand to her mouth.

But neither Naia nor Hathach flinched.

"You are Jewish, of course, my lady," said Hathach, and Esther nodded as he drew nearer and spoke again. "My queen, there is more that Mordecai desires you to know."

"Tell me, quickly," she breathed. "What is it?"

"He urges you to speak for the Jews." Hathach paused, weighing his words. "He said you must go to the king and plead for the lives of your people."

Esther had no answer to that. Hathach and Mordecai and every other soul in the land knew that to enter the court of the king without an invitation meant death. The king had not called her to see him for more than thirty days, and she sent Hathach to tell Mordecai just that.

When Hathach came for the third time, Esther felt sorry for him. He bent under the weight of his news. Indeed, he looked as guilty as if he himself had ordered the death of her people.

Esther folded her hands and took a very deep breath.

"Do not be afraid, Hathach. Tell me what he said."

Hathach swallowed loudly. "He said to tell you that . . . that you will not escape simply because you live in the palace. You will be found out. He says also that if you remain silent and do nothing, God will send someone else. But you and all your family will be struck from the earth."

Esther bore the blow of the words in silence.

Naia whimpered beside her, for her worst dreams had just come true.

Hathach cleared his throat. The message was not done.

"There is more?" said Esther, her voice low.

"Mordecai says this." Hathach spoke slowly. "He says that you have been brought to your royal position for such a time as this."

These words brought a sudden calm to Esther. It wasn't strength, exactly, but it was a quiet in which she was able to gather her mind and still her shaken heart. She glanced at Naia, whose tears streamed down her small face, then at Hathach, white to his lips with the news of the danger now brooding over the head of his queen. Death and destruction for her people, a swift death for herself. Yes there was so much to fear.

Yet who else but God had brought her to this place? Who else had protected and kept her through every upheaval? She straightened in her chair and lifted her head.

"Hathach," she commanded, her voice low but sure, "tell Mordecai to gather all the Jews in Susa. Tell them to fast and pray for three days, and I will do the same. I and my maids—any that will join me. At the end of that time, I will go to the king. And if I die, I die."

When Hathach left the room, Esther turned to Naia and pulled her into a close hug, making her arms strong to chase away the fear that made the little girl tremble like a leaf in a storm.

"Naia," she whispered, "do not fear for me. I am in the hands of God, a God more powerful than any king on earth. I know you cannot believe in him yet, but I believe you will see how good he is. I am not afraid. Now go, gather the other maids and tell them all that has passed."

When Naia was gone, Esther knelt by the window where she could just see Mordecai's head where he sat at the gate. The challenge had come, the time when the burning secret of her soul would be made known to the whole world. Just that morning she had longed for Naia to know the truth of God, and now the whole empire would see. God would show himself to all as the good and gracious king he was. She could barely find the words to pray, but she knelt and lifted her fear and hope to the God who had brought her to this strange time and place.

A few moments later, the door behind her opened and her maids pattered in. Esther took a moment to compose herself, then turned to face them. Immediately, a small body knelt swiftly at her side.

"I will pray with you," whispered Naia. "You are my queen, and if your God has made you the way you are, then I think he must be beautiful and full of love. I will pray to him too."

Esther could not speak. The answer to one prayer knelt beside her, the answer to the other would come. She hugged Naia tight and closed her eyes.

devotional

I am an introvert. I am shy, and I don't speak well on my feet. I am like Anne of Green Gables who came up with just the right, snappy reply at three o'clock in the morning two days after she needed it. So I have no idea what prompted me to sign up during a summer academic program for a day of downtown evangelization. Speak to strangers about the truths I held most dear? Unlikely. Yet there I was on a hot Saturday afternoon in the south, herded onto a bus with my fellow students, bound for a downtown park.

We had received just a bit of training and a piece of paper listing a few conversation starters, but mostly we were on our own. We went out among the picnickers and bikers, wandering the paths between fountains and playgrounds and stopping anyone who was willing to answer a few "spiritual questions." I was startled at how many did. I expected to be brushed off, ignored, even rebuffed. Yet person after person stopped to listen then talk about what they thought of life and God.

But adventure awaited me just around a hedge where my brother and I found an older man sitting thoughtfully on a park bench. He answered our first timid questions politely. Then he countered with a few of his own. We answered and poked a bit further. He poked back, and soon we were embroiled in a discussion of spiritual truth that went far beyond a surface encounter.

I was jumpy as a cat at first, deeply nervous that I would say something wrong. I was so afraid that instead of helping this curious man in his search for God, I would hinder him with my fumbled words. But as time went on, as his questions and objections probed my mostly deeply held beliefs, I forgot myself and my stumbling tongue and just spoke what I knew to be true.

His questions were of suffering and truth, of God's reality in the midst of pain, of evidence of His presence in the world. These were things I had wrestled with every day in my quiet times, doubts I had debated in my little red chair on many an early morning. These were questions I had been forced to answer for myself, so when the time came to speak them, I found to my surprise that I was ready.

For almost an hour, my brother and I talked with the man on the park bench. My shyness, hesitation, and fear melted away in the blaze of the truth I yearned to share and my unexpected ability to do so.

Later that night, in my dorm room bed, I thought about the fact that, shy and weak as I was, the truth of God was solid within me, and I had spoken from that strength. I didn't dazzle that man with my sparkling personality or my witty repartee. Instead, I had communicated my faith in spite of myself with a love refined over many struggling years.

I had always wondered how the great missionaries found the courage to speak, especially when forced to choose between faith and life. I always imagined they must have a particular God-given talent fortified by an iron discipline. But that night I realized that the truth we speak under pressure is simply that which we have believed day after day.

The powerful words of evangelists and martyrs did not fall sudden from their lips. No one wakes up one fine day and decides, yes, today I am strong enough to confront the unbelieving thousands, or even die for God. When a sword is at your throat or a gun to your head, the answer you give will be the one you have practiced in all the quiet moments leading up to that one, pivotal moment of truth. It is the same in the small times when no danger threatens and some curious friend or talkative stranger asks about your faith. The answer you give will be the one your heart has spoken quietly to God, the truth you have embraced daily.

This is the sort of quiet certainty I see in the life of Esther—a daily cultivation of faith that made her ready to risk her life when "such a time as this" came knocking at her door. I believe she was able to agree to Mordecai's rash suggestion that she enter the king's chambers uninvited because she had decided over many long days of prayer that her life was not her own, but God's.

Hers was a living faith, and even when secrecy was required, her heart sought the Lord daily. Look at her final response to Mordecai: *Tell everyone to fast and pray, and I will too.* These are the words of a young woman for whom prayer was a first response, the answer to every dilemma. Her ready willingness to die for her people demonstrated a lifetime of trust in God. She couldn't have spoken those words so quickly and with such determination unless she had surrendered her heart fully to Him. God had brought her to this time and place for this purpose, and she trusted Him to see her through this situation.

How can we, as modern girls, be ready to answer His call in our own time? We've already talked about ways we can invite and cultivate the presence of God in our lives—the disciplines of Scripture reading and prayer, the pursuit of quiet and of beauty and grace. But there's also great value in making the effort to articulate exactly what we believe and hold to be true about God and our relationship to him.

There are so many days when I complete my quiet time and then life rushes in and there's so much to be done that God feels like just another check on my list. So I have made a practice of ending my devotions by stating exactly what I believe and what I want to become. I speak what I hold to be true: *Lord, you are the great Lover of my soul, and I yearn with all my heart to obey you today. I want to be your woman in my time. I choose you above all others. You are first in my heart, the treasure I prize above all else.*

These words define me and my daily approach to life as one of God's own. And I have found this to have been a common practice of God's people throughout the ages.

The Jewish people still begin their prayers each day with a declaration called the Shema, which begins, "Hear, O Israel: The Lord our God, the Lord is one. Love the Lord your God with all your heart and with all your soul and with all your strength" (Deuteronomy 6:4–5).

Christians down through the centuries have declared the Nicene Creed on a daily basis: "I believe in one God, the Father, the Almighty, maker of heaven and earth, of all that is, seen and unseen."

When you choose to affirm each day what you believe, it becomes part of you. It thrums in your blood and sinks into your bones and comes to you as naturally as breath. This is the truth you will whisper at the moment of your greatest testing.

So let me challenge you to speak out your faith. Affirm what you believe in the deepest part of your soul. Write a statement you can read aloud if it helps, or find a creed to give you words to articulate the truth on which your life is founded. Take the time to consider exactly what it is you believe and give voice to it every day. Then when someone comes to you with a question about your faith, when you are forced to say what you believe, you will be prepared because you have hidden the truth in your heart.

You, too, can be an Esther, ready for such a time as this.

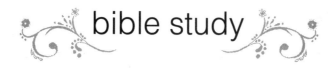

bible study

1 Peter 3:15–16

What must you always be ready to do? Notice what Peter says about "hope." How does this form the answer you will give? What must you communicate to the people you are trying to win to Christ?

Isaiah 52:7

How is the bringer of good news described? How can you bring the good news of God to your culture and time? What will you declare?

Luke 21:12–15

Who will give you the words to speak when you are taken before "kings"?

Matthew 12:33–37

If Jesus were to stand before you, what would come out of your heart? What would the words you speak say about the good or evil within you? What is the treasure within you?

Colossians 4:6

What do you think it means to "season" your speech? How can you prepare yourself to bring grace to everyone who hears?

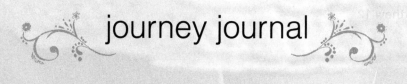

journey journal

chapter nine

Courageous Beauty

She was ready. At least, as ready as one could be knowing that death was likely waiting round the corner. With restless fingers Esther smoothed her robes one more time and adjusted the heavy braids that gathered her dark hair. With the heightened senses of the condemned, she looked around. Crimson flowers screamed beauty at her, the birds sang as if their hearts would break, and the air felt like the first sip of water in the desert. All of it precious and gorgeous and soon to be lost.

The three days of prayer had passed, and in a moment more, Esther would walk headlong into a swift death or miraculous mercy. She inspected herself one last time. Her one chance as she walked in the door to greet her husband was her beauty. She would dress as she had that first day, when his eyes came alive at sight of her and he had chosen her as queen. She would use every art she possessed to help him remember that he loved her.

Esther had decided as she prayed that this was the way to the king's heart. For three days she had begged God to show her how to approach the king. She remembered then that she had come to her place as queen because the first queen had rebelled. Vashti had scorned her husband, the king, refusing his request for her company and denying him the grace of her loveliness.

So Esther would do just the opposite. She would show up uninvited in the fullness of her beauty. She would bow with a sweet, proffered smile. Vashti had scorned the king, but Esther would offer him joy and invite him to a feast. That was where she would plead for the life of her people. She would not blurt out a wild, peremptory plea before the staring courtiers. She would save her request for the king alone. She would honor him with her secret and show him her trust.

Naia came in then, face flushed with her bustle and fear.

Esther whirled to her, just as jumpy. "Is the feast ready, Naia? Is everything in place?"

If the king extended the mercy for which she hoped, then she would whisk him straight away to a banquet, the like of which he had never seen. This would be a feast as lavish as her art could contrive, rich with every dish the king loved. She had prepared a table in the loveliest corner of her private garden. Musicians would play tunes to steal his heart, while the oil lamps would burn low and mysterious. Richly woven rugs covered the grass, and linens from the best markets covered the table. It was a feast fit for the greatest king on earth, and she intended to feed him heart and soul. If she could only manage to live that long.

"Yes, my lady. To the last detail."

"Well then," said Esther, letting out the breath she felt she had been holding for three days, "we can't delay anymore. I think it's time. Come here, my little one." Esther pulled Naia into a last motherly embrace. "No matter what happens, you must trust God to hold you, even as I have. He will go with us both."

"Yes," whispered Naia, unable to say more through her tears.

And with a last brush of Naia's arm, Esther rose, sighed, tucked a rose a little tighter in her hair and walked simply out the door. She refused any accompaniment. Should all go wrong and the king's anger fall upon her, she would not risk having anyone near her suffer punishment as well. No one but she must take responsibility for this daring intrusion. Hathach led her through the maze-like corridors and left her at the closed door. The entrance guards stared at her with shocked faces.

"My lady," whispered one, "I beg you, don't go in. Surely you know the law."

"I do," Esther said, with a feeling of unearthly calm now that the danger was before her. "Open the door."

And they did. The great wooden door creaked open as if in protest at Esther's dare. The sound of it echoed down the long, cool hall so that not a person alive in the room could miss the fact of Esther's presence. Silhouetted in the doorway, the late daylight dancing about her shoulders, she stood for a brief instant, gave herself into the hands God, and stepped forward.

Like rocks falling in a cave, her footfalls echoed from wall to wall, from the marble floor to heights of the lofty ceiling. She kept her eyes down in humility and also in fear that she could not make the long walk if she saw the king watching her approach. When she reached the foot of the throne, she whispered, "Please hear me, my husband," just loudly enough so the king could catch her words. Then she prostrated herself on the floor. Life or death was but a moment away.

How dare she enter without his invitation? His face flushed and his back stiffened. Would no woman obey him? She was just another Vashti, brazen in heart and bold in action, with no care to honor him before his lords or keep the customs of his kingdom. As her every step brought deeper silence to the hall, he fumed, concocting outlandish dooms for yet another rebellious wife.

But when she reached his throne, he saw her eyes, as different from the brash eyes of Vashti as day was from night. These were pleading eyes that swiftly dropped from his face in such abashed humility, he wanted to kneel beside her right then and lift her face so he could read the secret hidden there. And that whispered plea, not just to him as king, but as the husband she honored and loved. He felt in her gentle presence a kindness—a yielding that Vashti had never allowed him.

> **The joy in her face was like the morning sun in its rising.**

As the silence deepened in the room, he took his time and studied her. Esther's beauty had only grown, he decided. With a sudden stab, he saw that she was dressed as she was the first day he saw her, the day his heart leapt in joy to find so perfect a queen. What a sweet gesture! She lifted her eyes now, full of a wordless plea for his mercy.

And he found that he was willing to give it. Nothing but a matter of life and death could have forced her to this act. With a sudden rush of understanding, the king saw how his wife honored him with her presence, trusted him enough to save her. *I have missed her*, he thought in surprise. He held out his scepter, and the joy in her face was like the morning sun in its rising. She stood, graceful as ever, tears in her eyes, and touched his scepter. He stood and drew her nearer to his throne.

"What is it, my queen?" he whispered. "What is it you need of me? Whatever it is, you can have it! Even if it is up to half of my kingdom!"

"My dear king," Esther whispered back, "if it would please you, bring Haman and come to a banquet I have prepared for you."

"A banquet?" he almost laughed.

She glanced up at him from under those dark eyelashes, eyes arched mysteriously, and he felt the excitement of a secret in the invitation, the puzzle and fun of a feast worth the life of his marvelous queen.

"Bring Haman quickly!" he shouted, his voice tumbling over the heads of his dumbstruck lords, though his eyes never left hers. "So that we may do what Esther asks."

"This way, my lord," Esther said, and led the way to her gardens where all was grandly prepared.

When Esther walked into the garden on the arm of the king, Naia nearly squealed. Every maid at the table first went pale, then crimson with relief. So great was their joy, it seemed to charge the garden air with music. Laughter ran as free as the wine in the golden cups as the king and his counselor devoured the food and praised the queen.

Yet when the time came for Esther to make her request, she froze. As if a thousand voices screamed doom in her head, she knew that now was not the time to ask the king for the life of her people. Haman stared up at her, oily and expectant, as the king looked upon her with fondness and curiosity.

She stammered out another invitation. "If I have found favor with you, my king, please come once more to a banquet, with Haman. Tomorrow. And truly, then I will tell you my request. Please, my king."

The king lifted his eyebrows and, with pat of his belly, agreed. "I certainly won't refuse another feast." His voice grew serious. "But, Esther, you must tell me then what troubles your heart."

She bowed in acquiescence, and the king rose and left her garden. When he was gone, she sank into one of the chairs, limp as a wilted flower with relief to be alive and puzzlement at the strange turn of events.

Naia rushed into her arms. "He saved you!" she squealed. "Your

God must be very powerful, for you are alive."

And for the moment, Esther felt that all had been worth the dare because little Naia believed. Such joy was in her face. She stood straighter now, as if she was no longer afraid of the world, and there was a light in her eyes that Esther had never seen before.

"To bed with you," ordered Naia. "You are hungry and exhausted, and I will not let you sit up another minute. I will see to the arrangements for tomorrow's feast. You must sleep, and I think this God of yours will make everything clearer."

Esther did not object but went to her bed to enjoy the sweetest sleep she had yet tasted. And while she slept, God crept into the heart of the king and set the stage for the drama to come.

While Esther slept and the whole Jewish nation prayed, the king was restless and wide awake. Perhaps his queen's concern weighed on his mind. Perhaps he felt vaguely troubled by Haman. Whatever the cause, he woke his servants and demanded that they read the chronicles of the kingdom to him.

The tale they read that night was of an upright, loyal subject named Mordecai. Months before, Mordecai had overheard two men plot to murder the king. He rushed to Esther, and she sent Hathach straight to the royal counselors, so the life of the king was preserved.

"What was done to honor this noble man?" the king demanded.

Before the scribe could speak, Haman entered the chamber to ask a dark favor. But before he could say a word, the king demanded what should be done to honor a man in whom he took delight.

Haman never thought for a second that such a man could be any but himself, so he made an extravagant suggestion. "For the man the king delights to honor, have them bring a royal robe the king has worn and a horse the king has ridden, one with a royal crest placed on its head. Then let the robe and horse be entrusted to one of the king's most noble princes. Let them robe the man the king delights to honor, and lead him on the horse through the city streets, proclaiming before him, 'This is what is done for the man the king delights to honor!'"

"So let it be done!" cried the king. Go at once. Get the robe and the horse and do just as you have suggested for Mordecai the Jew, who sits at the king's gate. Do not neglect to do anything you have recommended."

Haman nearly swallowed his tongue. Unable to speak without protesting the command of his king, he simply bowed in obeisance and left the chamber, turning increasingly purple in rage with every step. He summoned Mordecai to the palace. Then he saddled the king's horse, wrapped Mordecai in the king's robe, and set the royal crown on his head. Then Haman led him through the streets of the city, calling, "This is what is done for the man the king delights to honor!"

Evening hushed the garden. A tent was draped amid the trees, lit with the fluttering light of a hundred lamps. Dim was the dusk light and soft the scented air. A feast to outdo even the first was set on the table within. This was the time, this was the hour when all would be won or lost.

When the trumpet sounded announcing the arrival of the king, Esther felt as if she couldn't breathe. *For such a time as this*, she thought as she opened her hands to welcome the king. She seated him in a throne-like chair and served him wine as evening grew thicker around them.

"Where is Haman?" she asked.

"Right here, my lady. My lord."

Esther cringed at the husky voice.

"Good!" cried the king. "A lovely feast again, Esther! Let us eat!"

Silence reigned for a time. Esther could not speak for the fear in her throat, while the men were satisfied to devour the food she had so carefully prepared. But finally, they sat back, mellowed and full. The king lifted his goblet to Esther, then sat a little straighter in his seat.

"And now, my queen, what is your request? What shall I give you? Again I tell you, even if it is half my kingdom, you can have it." There was a depth in his tone and care in his eyes as he watched his queen. Esther stood, heart in a patter of prayer, and walked with slow grace to the king. She fell at his feet.

"Lord, I beg of you, if I have found favor in your eyes, if it would please your heart, then grant me my life! This is my petition. Spare the lives of my people—this is my request."

She wept then and the tears were not false, for they were the culmination of days of prayer and danger and daring. Until now, she had borne it all with a dogged grit, borne the fear and grief at the evil wrought upon her people. Now she let the king see the aching of her heart.

> **"Spare the lives of my people—this is my request."**

For a moment, the king stared, mystified by her desperate plea.

Next to him, Haman leapt to his feet, his eyes two black pits of horror.

The king glanced up at his counselor and read the tale in his face. Instantly he knew, and his kind eyes went black with anger.

"My husband," cried Esther, "my people and I have been sold for destruction and slaughter and annihilation. If we had merely been sold as slaves, I would have kept quiet, because no such distress would justify disturbing the king. But we are to be killed. Save us. This is my plea." She knelt in silence, her plea made, her dare complete.

"Who is the man who would do this?" exploded the king with fury. His words were for Esther, but his eyes were fixed on Haman.

"He sits at the table with us, my king," Esther whispered. "Our adversary and enemy is this vile Haman."

Even before she spoke the words, Haman cowered beneath the gaze of the king, who watched him as a lion watches its prey. As if healed of blindness, the king saw the evil of the man before him. Unable to control his wrath, the king stalked out into the garden, leaving Haman alone and trembling with Esther.

Haman rushed to where Esther stood. "I beg of you, my queen!" he cried.

The anguished whine of the doomed man echoed out to the garden gate, and the king turned to see Haman grabbing at Esther's hands as she backed away, terror on her face. Like a lion protecting his mate, the king roared and lunged back into the tent, throwing Haman to the floor. "How dare you! Will you force yourself on my queen while she is in my house and I am with her?"

At the words, two guards walked forward and covered Haman's face. He was a doomed man.

"My king," whispered one of the guards, "you might be interested to know that Haman has built a gallows at his home, seventy-five feet high."

"A gallows?" The king was shocked. "Why?"

"To hang the man who saved your life, Mordecai the Jew."

The king's face was purple with rage. "Then hang Haman on it!" he shouted.

And it was done.

And so the great saving of the Jews was accomplished. Within hours, Mordecai was given Haman's position of power. Days later a proclamation went out declaring that not only could the Jews defend themselves on the dreaded day, they could attack any who tried to hurt them. The whole kingdom buzzed with the news, and the Jews soon found friends in every corner of the land.

When the original day of dread arrived, instead of death, there was feasting. Instead of grief, laughter echoed through the rooms of the palace. Esther laughed with her maids, feasted and danced, and when they had eaten their fill, she drew them to her feet and told them of her God.

Story after story she told of the one God who saved his people and kept them from harm. Esther watched the awed faces of the girls around her, saw the blazing light of Naia's eyes, and felt the glory of God dance around her like a song. *For such a time as this.* The words echoed in her mind as the joy of salvation filled the whole kingdom.

devotional

I was fresh out of high school, ready to change the world and determined to know God. So when a summer job became available with a ministry in the United Kingdom, I jumped at it. This was my chance for great adventure, to learn everything I wanted to know about my faith. I would drink tea, wander English streets, and discuss philosophy by the hour. But most of all, deep down, secret in my heart, I thought a summer of study might finally help me to feel God's love in the deep way I longed to, but never had.

Once in England, my main duties were to help run theology conferences, and I threw myself into the work. From dawn till dusk I pattered up and down cobblestone streets, listened to lectures, talked with conferees, and slept only occasionally. When I had time to think, I sometimes turned my thoughts toward God or took the pulse of my heart. I wasn't sure if I felt any more loved, but I was hearing so much about God, I thought surely that must count for something.

But after two months of poring over worldview tomes, writing papers, and listening to countless lectures, I woke one morning and realized that I felt farther from God than I ever had. All the theology I had studied had failed to touch my spirit with the warmth I craved. I lay in my bed in the dawn and felt so barren in soul, I wasn't sure I could finish the summer. I wasn't even sure I wanted to know God anymore. He seemed distant and complicated and unwilling to meet my girlish need for love. When I finished my work that day, I nearly ran back to my room.

I lived that summer in a ramshackle old country house made over into student housing. Good bones kept it standing, but its joints were all out of place and evident in odd staircases and tipsy attic rooms. But at its heart there glowed a narrow, homey kitchen crammed with mismatched teacups and a window that let in the sunset as I cooked. This became my refuge in the evenings, and most days I was joined by Aptin who cooked with me. Aptin was a professor who commuted to London. He had escaped from Iran when the shah was overthrown in 1979. We both got home late most nights, and we talked while he grilled salmon or made a soufflé. I loved his stories, and he distracted me from my student's fare of eggs and toast. On this particular night, though, my budget and soul were both so tight, I made plain oatmeal and just passed him as I headed upstairs with my dinner tray.

"Wait," he said, in his high voice and British accent, "I have found a new place in London, so I'm moving. I'm throwing myself a going-away party in the garden tomorrow night. I'd be so happy if you could come."

I had two days off, and even if I planned to spend them having a nervous breakdown, I couldn't offend my friend. I nodded my acceptance.

I woke the next day mad. I hated myself for struggling spiritually. I resented the teachers I had trusted to bring me closer to God, and who (I felt) had put up academic walls between me and His love. And I was furious with God Himself for leaving me to bumble about in darkness. By evening, I was fit company for no one, but I forced myself to go downstairs for the party. My heart was in my toes.

But one step outside, and I couldn't help but smile as I had stumbled into a fairy-tale feast. There in the prim English garden were three tables heaped with food like a pirate's plunder. Aptin must have raided every grocer in town! The first table was filled with thirty different cheeses amid mounds of breads, olive pates, and cracker stacks. Three giant bowls of fruit graced the next, full of grapes, pineapple, and tiny English strawberries, leaves and stems intact. The third held cordials and drinks galore. As my feet sank into the grass, Aptin hurried over to shake my hand with a smile.

"Oh, I am so glad you came! It's a perfect night for a feast. Fill as many plates as you can."

Somewhere between the brie and the cordial, I forgot to stew over my own troubles. There was simply too much to enjoy. I found a seat under a gnarled apple tree where the light was honey and gold through the leaves. The sun was on the horizon, and everything in the garden glowed—poppies and roses, the red stone walls, the rich wood of the worn tables. A merry group of housemates joined me beneath the tree, and an undeniably hobbit-like air descended upon our feast. Night grew as we lingered, and a warm, hushed darkness slowed our breath and refreshed our bodies. Bugs chirruped. Stars blinked. We chatted to the clink of plates refilled and glasses brimmed again. When sleepiness finally came, I climbed slowly up to bed.

The minute I opened the door, my earlier struggle sprang from the shadows. I clearly remember the way I tensed then. But even clearer, I remember the peace that came suddenly and relaxed my fear. Darkness passed me by, and I sat down on the edge of the bed, shocked at my lightened heart. The silver light of the moon fell full on my face, and out of the blue, I knew God loved me. Grace cradled my heart, and doubt seemed like a vanquished ghost. And it was all because I had tasted a bit of God's beauty.

Beauty, I realized that wondrous night, has the power to reveal God's presence. God isn't just a thought to be known; He is a joy to be sung, a feast to be eaten, the Great Delight of the world. God's love is felt in friendship. His joy sings in the wind and spices our feasts and glimmers in the golden sunsets. He made the cadence of the seasons, the crunch of apples, and the touch of friends to reveal His eternal goodness.

Sometimes, in my eagerness to know God, I have tried to draw closer to Him by thinking all the right things and reading all the right books. If you try to know God just by thinking about Him, you will soon find yourself with a dry and thirsty soul. You can say the right things and know all the right truths, but if you miss the winsome delight of God, you will miss the true essence of His being.

Esther understood this. Esther knew that beauty could help her speak truth. When Esther had to convince the king to change his mind, she used a feast to win his heart. She made herself lovely, threw him a party, and delighted the king as richly as she could. The fact that Esther did this may seem a small point in the overarching story of how she saved her people, but I think it's crucial. I think Esther's skill in bringing life and beauty to others won the battle for the king's heart and saved the lives of her people.

Did you know that you, too, can influence people simply by making the world a more beautiful place? With every word you say, every song you sing, the home you present to others, the teatimes or feasts or parties you throw communicate to the world what you believe to be true. My mentor, Phyllis, says that beauty in hospitality communicates worth to the people you invite. Beauty tells people that they are precious to you and to God, and that the God you serve is delightful.

Beauty really could change a culture because it is such a winsome way to communicate truth. In reading the story of Esther, I began to see what a model she is for anyone who wants to be a world changer. I want to win hearts, I want to fight for God, and I have realized I can do this by being a maker of beauty.

"Taste and see that the Lord is good," David says in Psalm 34:8. So I've decided I will invite as many girls into my home as I can, and I will serve them cream scones with jam, and hot tea in real china cups. I will make feasts for my family and friends. We'll gobble up potato soup and hot herbed bread and know the goodness of God. I will linger in conversations with lonely people. I will fill my home with music. And I will reach out to the poorest people I know by inviting them to a big family meal with candlelight and conversations late into the night.

The end result of my summer in England was that I finally understood that God is not merely a thought I must think or a proposition I must know. God is my Lover and Maker, my Friend and Counselor. He reveals His goodness in the tangible wonder of His creation. Truth is vital, of course. Esther had to save her people. But if truth is presented coldly, without love and beauty, or it can ring empty to the soul. Being a woman of God doesn't mean just knowing the right things. It also means being thoroughly alive to the joy and beauty of God.

Two months of study couldn't give me what one night of feasting could, because beauty known and people loved are great ways that God offers His hand to us while we sojourn here on earth. By loving, by feasting, by reaching out and touching His beauty, we take hold of His hand and let Him fill our hearts with joy.

And we can offer that joy to others. I don't even know if Aptin shared my faith, but somehow he had grasped a heart of celebration, the heart of Esther, the heart of God. The longer I walk with God, the more I am aware of the joy that fills his soul. I feel his laughter, I remember that the new heavens and earth will begin with a feast (Revelation 19:6–9). And I realize that each meal I serve is a small reflection of His goodness, an offering of beauty to win the hungry hearts of my time.

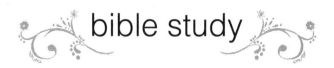

bible study

Psalm 36:7–9

How does the psalmist describe God's delights? Listen to the imagery. "River of delights." "Fountain of life." How does this shape your perception of God's character? Have you tasted His delight?

Exodus 28

Read this passage and ask yourself why God was concerned with such intricate artistic detail in His tabernacle. What do you think He wanted the priests to be so beautifully attired? What might that beauty communicate about the God they served?

Psalm 19:1–6

What does nature tell us about God? Throughout the books of the prophets, whenever God wants to convince people to believe in His power and goodness, He tells them to look at creation. Why? What does beauty speak about God?

Matthew 12:33–37

If Jesus were to stand before you, what would come out of your heart?
What would the words you speak say about the good or evil within you?
What is the treasure within you?

Colossians 4:6

What do you think it means to "season" your speech? How can you prepare
yourself to bring grace to everyone who hears?

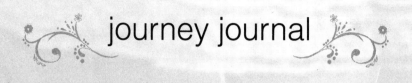

journey journal

part four

Ruth

chapter ten

Claiming the Light

Can a child know, in a single instant, a god of whom she has never heard?

She can if he is a light that rescues her. On a night of fierce black and fiery red, the light first came to me. I remember red most, crimson in the frenzied eyes of my neighbors at their festival sacrifice. Red burned in the cheeks of the glassy-eyed priests as they chanted, crazed, for the sacrifice to be presented. Then there was the red blood of the animals themselves as it was spilled and scattered over our bowed heads.

We had all come, the whole restless city, to the high place of our stone-faced god, Chemosh. Shadows striped the temple arches as the procession entered, the doorways marching before us, each filled with a formless dark. I could not look up for fear of the robed priests, shaved and solemn, emerging from those shadows with faces as lifeless as the stone idol they worshiped. Crouched next to my mother in the great temple hall, kneeling with hundreds of others, I felt the heat in the room rise in chorus with the voices as they swelled from a hum to a barely contained scream.

I remember the cries of some animal, rending cries, remember the way my mother clutched me to her side. I remember strongest my sudden panic as the priest flung something out over us. Red spattered my white tunic and streaked my hands as I tried to wipe it away. I felt a presence in the room, hot like guilt, inexorable, and I knew terror for the first time. I sprang from my mother and ran. I leapt over bowed backs and skirted the open spaces where priests swayed. I hugged the stones of the hall, the granite scraping my face as I edged my way, unseen, out of the temple and into the night. There I looked out at a sky as black as my mind, cold and empty.

But through it shone the moon. The beam of her light was clean, untouched by any stain or shadow. She pulled my eyes to her, and I walked forward and stood in her brightness. She washed me with the clarity of her light. Far above, beyond my touch, she cast a light that could not be sullied by human touch. Her height was a comfort, a shield about me. My breath slowed, the hot fist that grasped my heart was loosed, and suddenly I knew.

Beyond this small, hot place, beyond that dirty little room filled with aching people, beyond this life, there was a world of brightness, a house of the heavens filled with light. Beyond the frenzy was a high untouchable beauty that could not be changed by the sordid spells and spilled blood. And at the heart of that light was some face, some mind whose thoughts I could not yet think and whose eyes I could not yet see. Yet I knew it was the source of all good.

From that hour on, I clung to the light.

Can a tiny girl understand that idols are no more than the wood or stone of which they are made? Can she hold onto that conviction into womanhood? Yes, if she is a girl caught in a prison of a life whose gates are the idol temple at which her family worships. Yes, if ever and always some gleam of the light calls her to hope, some shield keeps her from the darkness around her. Throughout the days of my girlhood, I felt the presence of that light. I refused to attend the festival sacrifices. I sought out the moon and the stars at night. I prayed—if a wordless ache can be called a prayer— to the nameless light to make itself known to me. But as I came into my womanhood, and the sons of the families close to mine cast eyes upon me, I began to fear. I watched the men who might be my husband and drew back, burned by some quenchless dark in their eyes.

And then came Mahlon. He was clean. His eyes were clear. The light shone through them, and I had never seen that in a man before. Mahlon was a Jew and a merchant. My father did business with him, and I met him in our cellar, a cool, dusty place where my father grumbled good-naturedly with the merchants who stocked his store. I had come down one day for wine, but Mahlon drove all thought of the errand from my head when I saw him.

He stood so straight, was so civil to me, so gracious to my father. Most of the men my father did business with threw me half-interested glances from which I quickly turned. But Mahlon was different. Kindness was in all his words. I soon contrived to be nearby whenever he came for my father, and I imagined with joy that he lingered when I was present. One day we snatched a quick word before my mother or father could cluck their disapproval. I learned his name and his trade, heard that his father was dead, that he cared for his mother. He gave me the keenest of smiles before my father's voice sent me scrambling.

> **Kindness was in all his words.**

The very next day I met Naomi, the mother of Mahlon. She came, radiant, wreathed in smiles and bearing a small basket of fruit. She asked to see my mother. The wives and mothers of merchants must be friends, she said. So hearty was her laughter, so kind her gifts, so sunny her talk, that my mother soon loved her. A month later, I came into my mother's room just as Naomi was leaving, and she cast me an arch smile. "Ruth," she asked, "what do you think of my Mahlon?"

I blushed, of course. What girl doesn't when the name of the one she favors is spoken? Naomi merely smiled. My mother let out a clear, merry laugh behind me. I knew then that the two of them had matched up their children, and the matching suited my heart full well. I laughed then, too, for if my mother were willing, my father soon would be. The match was a fine one to their eyes. Mahlon was kind and respected, successful in the small shop he owned.

I soon found my great light had a name, and my life was changed forever. The change began when I told Mahlon of the light that had come to me when I was a girl, and that I saw this same light at times in his eyes. Then he told me of Yahweh.

I knew that Jews worshipped one god, but as Mahlon's wife, I learned the name of that God. I joined in the family worship, intent on learning the psalms and stories of Moses, the words of a God who called himself simply, "I Am." Slowly I came to believe that the nameless face whose beauty had called to me in my childhood was the God of the Jews. He was the source of Mahlon's kindness, the force of mercy that drove him, the reason his eyes were clear when all around him walked in darkness.

His mother, Naomi, became my teacher then. Mahlon would leave for his work, and the three of us women—Orpah, the wife of Mahlon's brother joined us—would draw together for a lively round of learning. Naomi was queen, and we her willing servants. She taught us all she knew of love, of the making of a gracious home, and she led us in worship of her God. Naomi had been many years exiled from her homeland, but in speaking to me of her God, she grew more brilliant than ever. We cooked and feasted, we talked and laughed, and in the light of that house, in the glow of the love, in fullness of that life, I knew joy.

Then came the breaking.

Swiftly, from one night to the next, all was lost.

A fever swept through our city, and Mahlon and his brother, Kilion, died.

We women sat silent in the house, bereft. Then came messengers with the news that Mahlon's business had been taken by men whose interests were tied up in his stock.

We were widowed and now poor, three women alone in a bustling city. We had nowhere to go. Naomi came down the day after we buried our husbands, her face like stone. She would go home, she said, back to the country she had left so long ago. We could choose to go back to our families or come with her.

Having lost our husbands, how could we now bear to lose the glorious mother we had known? There was no choice. We would go. We bid farewell to our families, packed small bags with only the most needed and most precious of our things, and left the house where we had come to life together. I felt like a homeless child stumbling blindly after this God I barely knew, still chasing after the light that kept me from fear.

As we walked, Naomi spoke of the land to which we journeyed. Our food was simple, poor fare after the feasts we used to enjoy. By the second day, Orpah's face was twisted with weariness and fear. That night, Naomi strove to turn us back. The journey and life ahead would be hard, while our families would keep us in luxury. When we were too weary to speak anymore, we fell asleep and waited for the morning to decide.

Naomi tried to make our decision for us. She crept from our lodging without a word while Orpah and I lay asleep. When we woke and found her gone, we wasted not a minute. Naomi was my only link to the life I had loved. I was desperate to get her back. We caught her at the place where she awaited a caravan just as the sun rose to noon in the sky.

I saw her first and could not walk on for the grief of the sight. Ever a woman radiant with life, Naomi was now a bent figure, darkened by the cloak she wrapped about her shoulders and the black veil that covered most of her face. Bereft of life, drained of laughter, when she beheld us her greeting was but a sigh.

"Oh, my daughters," she said as we knelt, each taking her frail hands, "I wish you had not come. I have nothing more to offer you. Go back to your families. I pray that the Lord will deal kindly with you, for you have been kind to me." She placed a hand on each of our heads. "And may God grant you rest in the house of another husband."

> **"I pray that the Lord will deal kindly with you, for you have been kind to me."**

We wept, broken at the thought of leaving her, torn between fear and hope.

"No," Orpah cried. "We want to stay with you."

Naomi took her hands from us then and stepped back, apart. Hardness came into her eyes as she spoke. Her tone was harsh. "Go. Now. Why should you stay with me? Do you think I still have sons in my womb to be your husbands? Go back, my daughters! I am too old to have a husband. Even if I married today and bore sons, would you wait until they were grown? Would you stay unmarried and unprotected? No, my daughters, it is more bitter for me than for you, for the hand of God is against me."

So final was her tone, so bitter the grief in her face.

Orpah relented. I watched, speechless, as she kissed Naomi and left us with her head bowed.

Yet I remained.

Unsure of what to say, muscles limp, I waited until Naomi took me by the shoulder and shook me. "Look," said Naomi, voice brittle, "your sister-in-law has left and gone back to her people and her gods. You should go with her."

I startled at the word "gods." And in a blaze of comprehension I understood the choice before me. There were two paths leading in opposite directions. One was to cling to all I had known, to my family and the gods they worshipped. The other was to walk boldly into a future shaped by a land I had never seen, a people who could not claim me, and all of it under a God whose light I had followed from afar.

My choice, I knew at last, was one of loyalty. Not to Naomi, but to her

God. All my life I had clung to the presence of a light that kept me from the terror of idols, that brought to me Mahlon, that set me in the joy and safety of Naomi's home. This light had comforted and shielded me, even when I did not know its name. I believed now that the light I loved was Yahweh, the God of Mahlon and Naomi, the source of all good. Would I now choose to follow that light into the unknown?

Until now, the light had always been outside of me, a goodness I beheld and followed but did not take as my own. It led, and I followed. It gave, and I was grateful. Never had it asked any sacrifice of me. My worship was cushioned by wealth, by the faith of a husband and mother much stronger than me. My marriage had sheltered me from the anger of my parents when I chose to worship the God of my husband.

But now, stripped of all that held and stayed me, the choice was mine. No other's faith would shelter me now. No extra grace of escape or wealth or ease would enable my response. There was only me, Ruth. Would I take this light for my own?

"Naomi," I said, "do not urge me to leave you."

Naomi sank down on a rock then, shoulders slumped, too tired to argue. I knelt again and took her hands in mine and waited until she looked me full in the face. Her shadowed eyes met mine, and it hurt me to see the lack of brightness in her gaze. But she looked steadily at me. She saw, I think, the joyous rise of my answer, the words that welled up like water from the deepest part of myself.

"Where you go, I will go. Where you stay, I will stay. Your people shall be my people, and your God"—I held the words on my tongue, savoring the strength of this choice, the mercy that led me to it—"shall be my God."

And the light was no longer a thing outside me, but a life within me, a strong beam of joy illuminating my heart. This light filled my thought so that my very eyes were changed, and I looked at Naomi from out of its splendor. The life of the world leapt within me, and the strength of ages was firm beneath my feet.

Naomi bowed her head and leaned into my arms. My declaration was final, and she knew it. She was no longer alone, and she wept as I held her fast. Clatter, clack, the rumble of the caravan echoed down the road. I shouldered my bag and stood, for the journey was upon us and I had made my decision.

"Well," said Naomi and stood beside me. Nothing more. But she leaned close to me as we began the journey that would take us both to a life and place beyond what we could see. I looked down the horizon as the landscape of my spirit changed and the road rose up before me. The light was strong in my heart, calling me to a new home.

I would follow.

devotional

I remember the moment with perfect clarity. A huge, squirming roach fell from the ceiling and landed with a light *thunk* on my shoulder. I leapt from the couch in an agitated dance, brushing my shoulders and back and shaking my arms until the awful creature fell to the floor, and then I committed insecticide. Heart palpitating, hands still shaky, I stopped and stood in the stillness of my room—and laughed. Just laughed.

What a way to begin a life with God!

My quiet time that morning had turned, to my shock, into a day of reckoning. I was a little surprised at the way God pushed my heart, demanding a full and final giving of myself to Him in a way I never had. Until that moment, I assumed I was about as thoroughly entrenched in the house of faith as anyone on earth. I was born to it and never really stepped outside its doors. I had, I knew, pushed as far past those doors as I could in the past year, craned my neck out into the air of doubt, and fought the household of faith pretty hard.

But then, it had been an agonizing year. My whole family had just been uprooted from a home we adored in Colorado to move to the humid wilds of Tennessee. This had been precipitated by a year of upheaval in which many of the things I thought were sure, crumbled. I lost a church family and community I loved. I went through a major crisis that left me emotionally shaken. My health failed, and I began a seven-year struggle to diagnose what was wrong. I had, I thought, every reason to hold myself aloof from God. If this was what He allowed to happen to those who loved Him, who had been obedient most of their lives, then I wasn't sure what I thought about Him anymore.

Yet throughout this difficult year, God had whispered to my heart. He wooed me in quiet ways and never left me alone. I felt His presence first in something that meant much to me as a writer—an epic story. J. R. R. Tolkien's *The Lord of the Rings* pierced my doubt with a picture of bravery and beauty. Here I saw a little hobbit who gave his life to fight against evil, who spent every drop of himself in holding to what is right, even when pain and loss had taken everything he had. His story whispered to my heart, prodding me to follow his example.

Then I began to read through the story of the Hebrew exodus in my quiet times. Daily, I was swept into the story of God's people when He called them out of Egypt and claimed them for His own. On the morning of my roach encounter, I read Deuteronomy 10:22, and the words "hold fast to your God" called out a challenge to me.

I had a weak-fingered grip on God.

When suffering called His goodness into question, when loneliness made Him seem far away and uncaring, I allowed myself to doubt and loosened my hold on faith. This verse made me realize I had to make a final choice. If I wanted to truly belong to God and live my life for His kingdom, if I wanted to be a Frodo in my world and fight the darkness, I had to cling tight to my God. And I had to declare my allegiance to the world.

Ruth's vow to Naomi was just that sort of declaration.

I believe God had whispered in Ruth's heart from childhood, and that her vow to Naomi was the culmination of her response. Her words of devotion were her full and final assent, her declared acceptance of a love that had wooed her for many years. I believe God calls us all from childhood, that He whispers in our hearts, nudges us to think of Him even when we are far away.

A friend of mine who came to Christ in her thirties said that though she delayed her decision, she knew God had been with her since she was a child. "Through every dark time and disaster of my teenage years, and all the wild things I did in my twenties, I knew He loved me. I knew He was waiting. I was the one who stood apart. But the night I accepted Christ, I knew in my heart that I had to decide. Now or never, make my choice and live it out for the rest of my life."

I believe we all must arrive at that moment. I think it's crucial that we, like Ruth, speak out our decision to follow, love, and seek God the rest of our days. For those who have come to faith later in life, the call is clearer—there was an old life, and now there's a new. For those who, like me, grew up well schooled in all aspects of faith, the urgency can seem absent. You may have a sense, even, of having come by faith in the same way you came by the color of your eyes. You had no part in the choosing.

Yet the call does come. No woman who says she will love and follow God can do so secondhand, by casual acceptance of the faith of family or friends. You cannot love God with half yourself and expect Him to inhabit every moment of your life with holiness and miracle. If you want to be a true follower of God, to blaze with His light in the darkness of your time, then at some point, you will have to answer His call. The moment of choice will come when the hosts of heaven lean down to hear your response.

As I sat on my little couch in my garage apartment, I made a promise to "hold fast" for the rest of my days. Until that point, I had believed in God, but I didn't trust Him. I feared pain, I doubted the future, and I allowed myself these reserves from faith, saying it was only fair—*I love you God, but I must hold onto that deepest part of myself. I want to maintain some sliver of control over my heart in order to limit the amount of abandon you ask of me.*

Finally, that morning, I opened my hands and let go.

I looked fully in the face of my God. I acknowledged that He was the truest, most beautiful thing I had ever found and that I would cling to the truth of His love even in the darkness. Never again would I allow myself to withdraw from Him, to withhold any part of my heart from Him. The choice was made. The roach fell. And I have walked with God ever since.

The beautiful submersion, the utter giving of your soul to the vast goodness of God means you will walk with Him in a different way from that moment forward. I soon found that my choice changed the way I looked at life. Now all things in my life came from, and were lived to, God. And I began a lifelong process of relinquishing more and more of myself—my time, my loves, and my needs—into the hands of the One who made me. It didn't happen all at once. But my choice opened the floodgates. My choice, spoken from the heart, sparked a work of creation that will continue right into the new heavens and earth and the someday world for which we all hope (Philippians 1:6).

Ruth's vow set the stage for a life of faith. My choice did the same. If you want to walk the way of Ruth and be a woman of God, then you must make the same choice. The great light of the world waits to fill every part of your life, just as it did Ruth. So choose today and be filled with a light that will never fade.

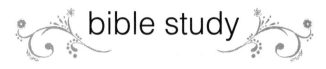

bible study

Deuteronomy 30:19–20

What choice did God set before His people? Why was it important for them to declare which way they would follow? What was the result of their choice?

2 Timothy 1:7–8

What has God given to His people? Are you ready to join in the "suffering for the gospel"? Why or why not?

Matthew 10:31–33

Why is it so important that we openly confess our belief in Christ?

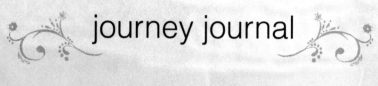

journey journal

chapter eleven

To Walk in Darkness

"Call me Mara." Naomi's voice quavered as she gripped the hands of the old friends sitting at her table. "My name is 'bitterness' now, for God has dealt bitterly with me."

Ruth, hard at work in the next room, set her lips tight. She paused an instant to listen for the mournful sighs that always followed as friend after friend bemoaned their sister's awful fate. There—a veritable chorus this time. Teeth set hard together, Ruth turned back to her third cleaning of the floor. Two weeks she had been in this home. Two weeks she had worked from dawn till dusk to scrub away years of abandonment. Layers of dust covered every surface, spiders lurked in every corner, and nothing was as she had expected.

Ruth's had been shocked by the commotion at Naomi's return. In Moab, Naomi and her sons had been but a few foreigners in a city teeming with thousands from far-off lands. Here she was old blood and known throughout the country. To Ruth it seemed her primary job now was to answer the door to a steady stream of old friends and forgotten neighbors hungry to know what had befallen the splendid family they once knew.

She was taken aback at the way they all stared and then passed her by as if she were mute. Their guests would shoot her a quick glance and stop, startled by Ruth's calm eyes and outlandish dress. With grace, she would bow, step back, and open the door so that Naomi could call her mournful greeting. Then the lot of them would huddle together, their commiseration punctuated with muffled sighs and covert glances. Ruth knew she must bear this. She spoke their language and worshiped their God, and she knew that over time they would come to see her as Naomi did.

But nothing had prepared her for the great despair of Naomi. On their journey, Naomi maintained a stoic if sad and quiet demeanor. But now silence had become a sickness in her. Unless she was receiving visitors, she would not talk or even cry. Most days she sat in a corner, cloaked in black, taking no interest in setting the house to rights. She seemed to feel no hunger. The woman who once ran her house with a hand of iron and soul of gold now watched with vacant eyes as Ruth cleaned and cooked.

Once the sun to Ruth's world, Naomi was now lost in a black place where no light could reach her. Ruth thought she understood. For Naomi, this had been a house bathed in the laughter of her sons, a shelter made by her husband. Every panel, board, and stone cried out to Naomi of the men to whom she had given the whole of herself. Now they were dead, and her light had died with them.

Ruth had no choice but to take what she had and set to work, even as days passed into weeks and the women of Bethlehem streamed in and out the door and Naomi mourned in the shadows. Today, she was determined to rout the last of the spiders. She had plans for each inch of space—shelves next to the fire for dishes, a garden in the courtyard, a jug of flowers for the table. She wanted to paint something pretty on the old walls, but that would have to wait.

Her concern today, the worry eating at her stomach even as she swept, was food. They had almost run out of money. A meager pack of clothes, a few treasures, a little food—this was all they had brought from their old life. Their meals had grown simpler by the day. Ruth would have to find some way to support the two of them.

She rolled her eyes as another knock sounded on the door. Pushing the stray hairs under her scarf, she opened the door and another woman bobbled in. Ruth returned to her work. Another spider jumped.

"Call me bitter," she heard Naomi's refrain rise again from the next room.

"Call me weary," Ruth yearned to yell back, for she was.

The rest of the day she spent scheming. She supposed could sell her mother's necklace, the last tie she had with her family. But what merchant would give her a fair price? Or she could offer herself as a cook and maid. But what good housewife would hire a Moabite?

That night, after the chattering neighbors had all gone, as Naomi lay on her bed in the same, unbearable quiet, Ruth lay on her pallet in the darkness, tormented by questions. Where was her hope in this new place? If the women looked askance upon her, how much more the men among whom she had thought to find a husband? How would she get food? Weariness finally forced her to sleep, but she turned fitfully, dreaming now of the wild night with the idols, of a face in the moon, and of herself straining to see if the face was kind.

"Ruth? Ruth!" A garbled scream jolted Ruth awake.

The scratch of Naomi's blankets came to her ears as the old woman thrashed in the darkness on the other side of the room. Ruth leapt up and knelt by Naomi's side, untangling the blankets and pulling the woman into her arms.

> **Where was her hope in this new place?**

"Shh. I am here," she said.

Naomi clutched Ruth's arms with claw-like fingers, and neither spoke any word as Naomi's grief burst its dam at last. When she could not weep anymore, Naomi laid still and fever hot against her daughter-in-law.

"Ruth, I can see only darkness." Her voice was stripped to a whisper by her tears. "My sons and husband are gone, and the God I honored seems far away. We have no food or money. I cannot even provide for you. Have I brought you to my home only for God to abandon us?"

Finally, the doubt was spoken. The deep darkness that hovered over Naomi and wearied Ruth's heart was given a name. Abandoned by God. Both women sat in the silent blackness of that thought. Had they been forsaken? Ruth felt the sway of her soul within her. Black, black was the night and darker still, the fear of her thoughts.

But suddenly, Ruth sat up straighter. In the wall above her was a tiny window, and through it she caught a beaming sliver of the moon. She thought of that wild night when the light had first called to her. She thought of Mahlon's face and how she had seen the light there. She remembered the last time she held Naomi like this, the day of her vow, when she had claimed the light of life as her own and taken Yahweh for her God.

Now the surety of her choice, the bold affirmation of her words echoed down from that day and into the darkness of the little room. Either God, in all his light, was with them or he was not. The choice tonight was no different than the choice on the day of her vow. Again, Ruth chose to trust the light of Yahweh.

She held Naomi tight. "Do not fear," she whispered in the dark, "God has not forsaken us. I know it. Naomi, he has given us each other. You were a light in my darkness, and now I will be a light in yours. Don't be afraid."

And she held Naomi until both of them slept.

When dawn's opal light lit the window, Ruth rose. She would foray out to the fields today. It was at least a sure way to get food. She knew of the Jewish law that allowed the poor to glean the remains of grain after the harvesters had cleared the ripened fields, and harvest time had come to Bethlehem. She would become a gleaner, on a treasure hunt for grain and the goodness of God along with it. She was dressed before Naomi could rise, and Ruth kissed her on the cheek before she went.

"I'm going to be a gleaner. I will be home at nightfall. Do not fear, my mother. God will take care of us both."

Ruth was afraid to venture outside as a foreign woman, despised and alone, but the sunshine was like tonic to her spirit. She did not realize how starved she had been of open air, how long she had been cooped up in the shadows. She walked in free stride through the shimmering barley carried by the wind, her eyes filled with the light of day. She lifted up her face and was glad. She did not even hesitate when she saw the workers deep in the harvest fields. She chose a corner where there were many women, where good humor burnished the faces that lifted and stepped in the dance of cut and glean. Then she went to the foreman to request permission to join the gleaners.

"Please," she began and held out her hands, head bowed, "may I join the women gleaning the grain?"

"Who are you?" barked the foreman, a sturdy, muscled man, his skin leathered by years of working in the sun.

"I am Ruth, the daughter-in-law of Naomi. We have just returned to Bethlehem and have no store of food."

"Ah, yes," said the man and raised an eyebrow as he scrutinized Ruth's face. "My mother knows Naomi. We heard of your return. Yes, yes, of course, go follow the women."

Ruth bowed in thanks and hurried to find a place among the women who worked, their backs bent, faces down, hunting the fallen grains of barley like tiny gems on the ground. A tiny ache burned in the small of her back after just ten minutes, but Ruth did not look up or around, only followed the women in their hard work. They did not deign to notice her much, though she felt a few stares take in her foreign clothes and complexion.

This was hard work, and Ruth wondered how long her strength would hold out. But she threw herself into the effort and was glad for the exercise. Step and bend and pick and sort. Like music the movement entered her muscles. *Blessed be God*, went the beat of her heart and the bend of her arm, and the light of God filled her as she stooped and stood and her shawl swelled with the grain that would keep her and Naomi in life.

Bless the day, boomed the heart of Boaz, in time with the hoofbeats of his horse. A sea of ripe grain rippled before him. The open sky blazed blue for harvest, and the faces of his people glinted up at him in greeting.

"The Lord be with you!" he shouted. He relished the laughter that rose to meet him.

"And the Lord be with you!" they answered and grinned up at the master whose sturdy height and strength was matched only by the kindness of his heart.

Boaz leapt from his horse and strode to greet his foreman. "It seems a blessed day, Jacob. Yahweh smiles on our work," he said, his arm on the other man's shoulder. "How goes it?"

Jacob gave his daily report on the progress of the reapers.

Boaz shielded his eyes against the sun to watch the bobbing backs of his men, and then turned to the bent figures of the gleaning women who followed in their wake.

"How many women this year, Jacob? Tell my maids to be diligent, and for the rest, I hope they glean plenty for their families."

"Nine, with the women you hired. We had an extra join this morning. She—"

Jacob was cut off as Boaz grabbed his arm.

"Who is that woman? The young one there on the farthest edge? I don't recognize her. Her dress is a little . . . different."

"That's Ruth, the one I told you just joined today. She is the daughter-in-law of Naomi. Quite a story, that. Naomi lost her husband and both sons to illness, but this Ruth insisted upon staying with her instead of returning to her family. She came this morning and asked if she could follow with the other gleaners. She's hard-working, I'll give her that, though I doubt I've ever said a good thing of a Moabite before."

The rise of Jacob's expressive dark eyebrows was lost on Boaz. Hand still shielding his eyes, he watched this Ruth. Neither to the right nor left did she turn. She simply bent and picked and moved with a determined set to her face. Yes, he had indeed heard the story of Naomi and Ruth. Moreover, he had pushed the gossips to tell it full. The old women went so far as to claim that Ruth had taken Yahweh for her God.

To Boaz, this was marvelous. Always, he had felt that the kindness of his God should draw all people to Israel, and here was a woman who saw that too. What a heart she must have! What faith! He must make sure she knew how welcome she was.

> **What a heart she must have! What faith!**

His sights set on Ruth, Boaz strode away from his foreman and made straight through the fields. Closer now, he saw the crimson of Ruth's face and heard the quick breath she took as she stepped and bent to retrieve the precious grain. She was intent on her task and did not notice him standing behind her. He bent and touched her shoulder.

"My daughter," he began and stepped back as she startled and hastily stood to greet him, her head bowed. "I am Boaz," he said, "the master of these fields. I am so glad you have found your way here."

She lifted her eyes to him now, and he saw they were warm like the summer-kissed earth and wide with the shock of his presence.

"My daughter," he said again, feeling the fact of his years and the boyish leap of his heart in one great tumble within him as he looked on her, "do not glean in another field, but stay in this one, with my maids, where you will be safe. Walk after them, and they will help you learn the way of it. I've told the servants not to bother you. When you're thirsty, please, drink freely of the water the servants draw, just over there."

Wider and wider those eyes grew in the dark oval of her face. He caught the glint of a tear before she suddenly knelt at his feet, hand against her heart, and said, "Why do you show me such favor? I am a foreigner. Why do you show such kindness to me?"

Boaz drew her back to her feet, the kind smile so beloved by his people lighting his face. "I have heard about you," he said simply. "I've been told all that you have done for your mother-in-law after the death of your husband, how you left your father and mother and country to come to a land you did not know." He stopped to take a breath, and his eyes dropped down now and his voice took on a hushed, gentle tone. "May the Lord repay what you have done. May you be richly rewarded by the God of Israel, under whose wings you have taken refuge."

The tears in her eyes welled openly now, and a relieved joy filled and lined her face. Flushed with her dusty work, worn by the sun and breathless as she was, he thought her lovelier than any woman he had ever seen. She wiped the tears from her face, laughed, and put her hands together.

"You have comforted me," she said in a broken, happy voice, "and though I am not even a servant of yours, you have spoken so kindly to me." With a last bow, she turned and went back to her work.

The world whirled around him, as it never had before. Boaz felt lost as a child, as if some great hand had shoved him off balance. He turned and strode back to the tent where his foreman waited. But the radiance on Ruth's face was all he saw.

Ruth bounded in the door just as night suffused the sky.

"Naomi!" she called and ran to the fire where the old woman stooped. "God has not forgotten us."

She heaved a large bag of grain onto their rickety table, and the wealth of it spilled over the wood. Naomi stood and picked up a few of the barley grains, eyes like two suns in her face. This was enough food to last them a week, and this was but the gleaning of a day.

"And I have this, too," crowed Ruth, taking from her tunic a small packet and handing it to Naomi. "Roasted grain. We ate it for the midday meal, and he urged me to bring this home to you."

Naomi threw her arms around Ruth and laughed.

"Where did you glean?" she asked. "Whose field did you enter, and who took notice of you?"

"His name was Boaz," said Ruth, and the whole of her filled with light like new dawn at the sound of his name. "He was kind beyond what I have ever seen in a stranger.

"God is indeed good to us."

He brought me to his table for the midday meal. He served me, and he urged me to stay in his fields throughout the harvest."

"God is indeed good to us," said Naomi, her voice quavering. "And, Ruth, he is a close relative of our family."

"He is?"

"Oh yes. He was always close to my husband. He has not stopped showing his kindness to the living and the dead. And now, you should do just as he says. Stay in his fields, and you will be safe. What favor he has shown you!"

Ruth saw in Naomi's smile a curve of something keen, but hunger drove curiosity from her mind, and soon the two women sat together by the small fire, filled by good food and even more by the prospect of help in the days to come.

In the satisfied quiet that followed, as the room filled with pleasant shadows and the fire leapt higher to greet them, Naomi turned to Ruth. "I am sorry for my darkness. I am sorry for doubting God. I hope," she said, and her voice broke a little with fear, "that I have not made you regret your choice to follow me here."

Ruth stretched a hand to Naomi. "I am surer than I have ever been. God cares for us. That is a marvelous thing to me still. And today, the kindness of Boaz, it was the kindness of God. We are not forsaken. Naomi," said Ruth, and waited until the older woman looked her in the face, "I am happy."

Night filled the air with hush, and Ruth was at rest. The fear of the night before was gone. Ruth felt sure that the light which brought her out of Moab would sustain and keep her through every change. Yahweh was a goodness that did not cease. Perhaps Naomi would know it again too.

That night, Naomi's sleep was peaceful and in the morning, as Ruth prepared to leave, a neighbor bustled in the door. "Mara," she began, but Ruth heard Naomi shush her and sigh.

"No, just call me Naomi," she said, her voice gentle. "For I am bitter no more."

devotional

When I first met Keri, I could have sworn there were two things, and two things only, in her head: boys and style. When she wasn't flirting with a boy, she was checking her makeup on the side. When she wasn't showing me her latest outfit, she was whispering about which guy in the crowd around us was cutest.

My first impulse was to roll my eyes and walk away. But Keri was the newest member of the small group of teenage girls I co-led with a friend from church. Walking away wasn't an option. So I got to know her instead.

At first, I saw her mainly at weekly worship and the study we held for the girls every other week. Keri didn't know anyone else, so she stuck pretty close to me at first. My initial impression only deepened by our interaction, and I openly told a friend that Keri was the shallowest person I'd ever met. I couldn't imagine she listened to a word of the teaching, and except for social purposes, I wasn't really sure why she was coming to our group.

What kept this girl with us? What was the root of her need to look perfect and be the center of attention? Soon I felt God nudging my heart. *Pursue her*, He whispered, *as I pursue you.* So—admittedly with a sigh—I did. I sat next to her whenever possible and invited her over to my house. I went to the harvest fair at our church as her special friend and next week had her over for a high tea at my home. Slowly, I got a glimpse into the heart of the girl I had coldly written off.

For example, I saw she loved babies. A little child couldn't come near but she was on her knees next to it, playing and cooing with a self-forgetful sweetness I have rarely seen. And she loved me. Her joy in my friendship was evident, and the delight she took in any outing we shared was childlike. She thanked me over and over for going for a drive or for the chance to bake cookies together in my kitchen. She raved about her discovery of tea in china cups.

She was still obsessed with boys. And she was still so self-conscious of her looks that we could barely walk through a restaurant without her asking me if she looked okay. I would pound my head (figuratively) in my quiet times and demand heaven to tell me if she heard even a morsel of the truth and wisdom I tried to share with her. But every time I felt disgusted by her lack of depth or foiled by her distraction, I felt a prodding in my spirit: *Push on. Be faithful to her as I am faithful to you.*

Then one night, after the church's annual Easter pageant, she sought me out. "Sarah," she whispered, as we crouched in a corner of the church, "I want so much to know Jesus. I've always wanted to be like you, to feel close to Him. But I don't know how, and I'm afraid. You have to help me."

I wanted to jump up and down in glee and hug her on the spot, but I contained myself (except for the hug) and assured her I would help her. I would show her Scripture and pray with her and lead her into all the delights of loving God. When I got home, I felt like dancing around my room. Two years of faithfulness had finally paid off.

I felt very much as Ruth must have felt when Naomi finally emerged from the dark night of the soul and changed her name from "bitter" to "blessed." My joy was probably similar to the elation Ruth felt when her hard work and her faithful choices brought her both food and favor. But I also think I felt as Ruth did during the long months of frustration leading up to her release.

For every brilliant moment in the life of a hero, there are a thousand faithful minutes in which nothing exciting or noble happens at all. There are countless days during which all the hero does is clean, work, and love in dull, daily rounds. Between Ruth's dramatic vow and the fairy-tale ending of her story, there were months of hard work and worry. There was a woman in deep depression to be cared for and an old house to be cleaned and meager food to be stretched by two poverty-stricken women. She must have wondered where this great and mighty God of Israel was hiding. She must have wondered if she would ever be loved again.

Yet instead of letting her doubts define her attitudes and decisions, she let her faith shape her heart. Ruth's vow to follow her mother-in-law and worship her God was not for dramatic effect. Her vow formed and defined her choices, her demeanor, and her life. When she claimed the God of Israel as her own, she claimed Him for every day and always. She gave Him her trust in good times and bad. She chose the road of faithfulness.

That is the choice you and I will also have to make if we want to follow God as Ruth did. Our trust in God has to be the kind that keeps us steady through times of joy and, equally, in times of dull, daily routine. Faithfulness like Ruth's requires a commitment of body, soul, and spirit to do what is right even when nothing exciting is happening in our lives.

My mother would say daily when I was small, "He who is faithful in small things will be faithful also in much." (You'll find this in Luke 16:10.) I cannot tell you how many times I heard that. When I was young, it usually had to do with housework I hated doing or schoolwork (like math) I was reluctant to complete. But as I grew, it became a theme of my spiritual life, a scripture that came to me over and over as I learned what it meant to follow God every day.

Faithfulness is an undervalued trait in our society. We live in a culture so steeped in the attitude of "get it now while it's hot" that we have a hard time waiting for anything. Even many believers think loving God means having their problems solved and desires provided the moment they pray about them. But true faith remains steady through feast and famine alike. A faithful heart is one that does not change allegiances, because it is founded on trust much bigger than any ups or downs we may be experiencing.

Ruth made a decision of faith that would carry her far beyond one fleeting moment or even the journey to Bethlehem. When things didn't turn out as she expected, she could have thrown down her broom and marched back to Moab. I could have thrown in the towel with Keri. But those who turn back will never taste the delights and rewards God brings. Nor will they be the ones whom God chooses to use in His story.

If we want to love God as Ruth did, we must learn to walk in faithfulness—spiders, barley fields, depressed mother-in-laws, and all. My time pursuing Keri taught me what the outcome of faithfulness might be. Yes, I was impatient and prideful at first. And if I had let those emotions rule me, I would have lost the chance to lead Keri's heart to the Source of all life. But I kept on, Ruth kept on, and both of us tasted the joy of faithfulness rewarded.

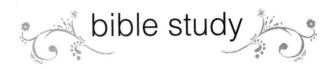

bible study

Psalm 37:3–7

What assurance can you find in this passage? Is faithfulness a dead end, or does it have a purpose? What will God bring if you trust Him?

Luke 16:10

What "little" things in your life require faithfulness? Can you imagine how they might prepare you to be faithful in much bigger things?

Isaiah 50:10

What does this verse say we ought to do when we are walking in darkness? What gives you the strength to be faithful when you aren't sure what's ahead?

journey journal

chapter twelve

Desire of My Heart

On the last day of the wheat harvest, Ruth and the other young women worked until the last golden rays of the sun swept low across the shorn fields. Laughter pealed out in time to the first gleams of starlight as girl after girl straightened and eased the ache from her back. The men ahead of them whooped and stomped. The harvest was in. Arms full of their last gleaning, the women cut a merry way homeward across the fields.

Ruth left her companions in gladness, brimming with joy at the fellowship they shared. In so short a time, great good had come to her through the kindness of one man and the people who followed him. In the fields of Boaz, Ruth had ceased to be a stranger in a strange land. The others now joked and whispered their secrets to her as they would with a woman of their own people. The men no longer stared at her or shunned her eyes at mealtimes. Instead, they all pressed in around her as neighbors. Finally, Ruth felt, she was home.

Tonight, as the voices of her friends rang up the street, Ruth leaned against the doorway of Naomi's house. A full load of grain scratched at her skin, waiting to join the gleaning already stored inside. The scratch and scuffle of Naomi's evening bustle came to Ruth through the door, and she smiled. Naomi was almost back to her old self now.

But Ruth lingered, eyes fixed on the far fields. She was almost sorry the work was over, however much her back cried for rest and her stomach for dinner. She would miss her golden days in the sun. But a sorrow much deeper pulsed within her heart, and her mind was filled with the strong face of Boaz. Straight and spirited, generous to all. Bold in his kindness and gentle in his words.

The fact that she loved Boaz came to Ruth now like grief. Her shy love of Mahlon was now lost in the shadows of her youth, and she had forgotten the feeling of it. The love she bore Boaz was much different, far deeper than what she had shared with Mahlon. Boaz claimed her respect, her gratitude for his protection, her joy in the vigor of his excellent life. Ruth felt her love for him in her bones and in her very soul.

But nothing could come of it. She was a foreigner, a widow, poor as the mice that skittered in every corner of her house. Ruth did not consider herself fit to be wife to the most respected man in town. No, tonight, in leaving his fields, she had left the circle of his life. She must simply bless God that she had known him at all and go about her way, however heavy her heart may be with unspoken love. She knew God's love a little better for knowing Boaz, and that would have to be enough.

Naomi was waiting, and Ruth she could delay no more. With a sigh, she turned her back on the far fields and entered.

Naomi glanced up from the fireside. "My daughter, welcome home. The last day of harvest is done! I have a good meal ready for us. You must be starved."

"I am." Ruth smiled and eased her load of grain onto the table.

"Go wash up," Naomi said, "and then we will go up on the roof to eat our meal. The day was a hot one, and the stars will be out."

Ruth went through to the tiny courtyard. The scent of old

> **She knew God's love a little better for knowing Boaz.**

earth and settled stone was strong as always, the fragrance intensified by the heat of the day and the following cool of night. Twilight shimmered over the surface of the water, and she plunged her hands into the bowl, as if she would touch the sky that had gathered there.

"I'm ready," she said, stepping back into the little room to dry her hands. Naomi stood with a tray at the ready and nodded toward the roof. Once there, they both stretched gladly out on the stones, their backs against the low wall that rimmed the rooftop. There was roasted grain and bread, a little olive oil, and a little wine. Ruth ate the work of Naomi's hands, and both were happy.

Both were also quiet. Ruth was simply tired, speech wrung out of her by the last hard push to glean and the faint regret that the golden days had ended. But Naomi sat in a taut, watchful silence. More than once, Ruth caught Naomi's eyes fixed upon her face. Eyes that searched, eyes that weighed. Ruth glanced a question back, but Naomi looked away.

They finished their meal and sat beneath the pageant of the stars. Ruth lifted her eyes to the mighty dance, diamonds awhirl in the blackness of the heavens. Never had she seen the stars like this in Moab. There the sky was hemmed by rooftops, the fearful dark above dimmed by the lights below. Here, Ruth thought the night to be full of joy. She gazed until her eyes were weighted with the beauty and she rose, heady with sleep.

"I am tired as I've never been." She smiled at Naomi. "I feel like a real farm girl, and now I will sleep like one. Thank you for the meal." She turned to descend the ladder into the house.

"Ruth, wait."

Ruth turned and found Naomi's eyes hard upon her again.

"Sit, Ruth. I need to speak with you."

Ruth sat close to the old woman, took one of her hands and pressed hard. "Is something wrong?" she asked.

"Not yet," Naomi said, taking Ruth's other hand in her own and holding them tight, "but it will be if I do not act. My daughter, my sweet Ruth. You have given so much to me and trusted so blindly. I must seek security for you, a life in which you are cared for so that you can be happy and all go well with you."

"But I am," protested Ruth. "Look at all the goodness God has brought us. We are fed and safe, and this house shelters us."

"I know." Fondness softened the fretful lines of Naomi's face. "You have done well. But you are young, and such things will not satisfy your heart forever." The old eyes met the young ones, and laughter played at their corners. "I have been thinking. We have a kinsman, you know. Boaz, in whose fields you have found such kindness . . ."

Ruth stiffened the muscles of her face lest her mouth betray her with a smile, or her eyes with a stream of sudden tears. The thought of Boaz quickened her heart, but she could not admit this. But Ruth's skin betrayed her. Like the youngest of girls, she flushed and saw laughter fill Naomi's face.

"Ruth, he is our kinsman, and by law, he ought to marry you and raise the fortunes of our family. You are the widow of one of his closest relatives—you ought to be his wife. I don't think either of you would find it hard."

Ruth grimaced. "Naomi, I am a Moabite. He cannot marry me. Why

217

would he want to?"

"Ruth, you belong to Yahweh. Boaz can marry you because he should and because he's in love. You must be blind if you don't see how much he likes you. Do you know you are the talk of every gossip in town for that very reason? Oh yes, they sit here all day. I don't miss a thing." Naomi paused and squeezed Ruth's hands harder and leaned closer to her face. "Ruth, you must trust me. You must do everything I am about to tell you because it is time you had a husband and a home. Will you do this?"

Naomi was her old self again, queen-like in her arch confidence, and a sense of reckless adventure came over Ruth as she listened to her mother-in-law. The gleam of a hope she never thought possible beckoned to her.

"Yes, I will."

"All right," Naomi beamed. "Go and get yourself as beautiful as you can. Wash, put on your best clothes, perfume yourself, and then go down to the threshing floor where Boaz will spend the night guarding his grain. Don't do anything until he has finished eating, but watch from afar. And when he lies down to sleep, go to him. Sit at his feet and uncover them. He will tell you what to do."

> **"I trust that God has set a great good before you."**

Ruth coughed, trying to force out the speech struck from her tongue by Naomi's daring instructions. "Naomi, are you sure?"

"Ruth, I have thought and prayed in my heart to Yahweh about this for many days. Boaz does not know how to approach you. Not because you are a foreigner, but because you are young and beautiful. He is afraid to look the fool or cause you embarrassment. Give him this chance. He is alone, where he can answer you without the whole village looking on. But you must act tonight. Go my Ruth. I trust that God has set a great good before you."

No longer sleepy but very much dazed, Ruth descended the ladder from the roof. She sat on the floor in her room and thought she could hear the beat of her heart in the silence. Terror and thrill leapt together in her heart. Terror at the boldness of this thing Naomi asked, fear that Boaz might break her heart. But also thrill that the one thing for which her heart longed might be granted. She sat up straight and decided she would not think, but just obey.

First she washed the grime and dirt of her work away. Then she knelt at the small corner chest that held the trappings of her life in Moab, the life in which she was pampered and kept, the perfumed wife of a well-to-do merchant. Not much remained from that time, but a few gems had survived her change in circumstances. Ruth clothed herself in a blue tunic she pulled from the chest—only in her best would she dare to confront Boaz. Next from the chest, she lifted a silken headscarf that slipped over her fingers like water. The purple of dusk glimmered in its folds, and she pulled it over her head, fastening the folds against her braided hair. Next, she drew out a bottle of cobalt blue. When the stopper was drawn, out leapt a fragrance like the scent of a summer evening, like starlight and sunset and roses brewed together and bottled in sapphire. She dabbed the oil onto her skin, then slipped three gold bangles onto her arms and stood.

Her mother-in-law waited by the door and sighed with joy at Ruth's loveliness. Naomi took Ruth's face in her hands and kissed her.

"Now go. God be with you," she said and shooed Ruth into the night.

His stomach was full, his harvest in, and the night bright with the stars he loved. So why did he feel as empty and starved as the meanest beggar? He had a crew of loyal men, a house full of servants, and a town that loved him. So why was loneliness a chasm at his back? Boaz grunted in irritation, turned over yet again on his pallet, and crossed his arms. This ought to have been the best night of the season. Until this particular harvest, he had been happy to spend a night under the wild sky, with the stars above him and the work of his hands locked safe at his back.

But tonight, peace, rest, and joy—a loyal pack usually—had scampered away and left him defenseless. He reasoned with himself. He chewed his lip. He counted stars in the hope that he would fall asleep, but to no avail.

The truth was that Ruth haunted his thoughts. Ruth's beaming face, her eyes golden with laughter. Ruth's low voice, her words ever soft. Ruth's loving heart, her touch gentle whether at work or play. Ruth was a want in him he could not escape. But she was as far beyond his reach as one of those stars.

For how could he marry her? Half his age, beautiful, a woman whom all the town held in high esteem. Why would she want to marry him? He could never ask her for dread of the rejection he was sure would come. And there was Japheth, the cousin who lived out of town, just barely closer in relation to Ruth and Naomi than Boaz. He could claim her first.

Yet the love of her colored his every thought. She was a ghost in his house, flitting from room to room, filling it with impossible dreams. She was a voice in his head when he felt alone, a phantom touch on his arm. He imagined her with him

> **A jewel, his Ruth, but one beyond his price.**

on Sabbath days, sitting at his table, filling his house with the brightness witnessed in the harvest fields. He pictured her at prayer. A jewel, his Ruth, but one beyond his price.

The sudden scratch of grass jerked him from his thoughts. He lay still a moment, listening, and heard someone breathe. To his shock, he felt a hand at his foot, and the blankets were pulled away. He sat up, startled, grabbing his staff and peering hard into the shadows.

"Who are you?" he rasped, hoarse with surprise.

Her voice was a whisper that came to him like a song. She had stepped right out of his heart and into his presence: Ruth. She crouched at his feet, her face lifted to his. By the starlight, he saw her eyes, but his mind was so full of her already, he saw her as plainly as if it were noon. He saw the pleading that lined her face and softened her voice, the humble bend of her head as the soft words fell from her lips.

"I am your servant, Ruth," she said. "Spread the corner of your garment over me, for you are my kinsman and redeemer."

He could not move, he could not breathe. Joy welled up in him like a river and flooded every nerve of his body. He knew the old customs, the old symbols—her plea to be covered was a request for marriage. She wanted him for her husband, old in body and boyish in heart as he was. He would never admit it in the daylight, but tears were on his face as he crawled to where she knelt and put his hands on her shoulders.

"The Lord bless you, my Ruth," he said. "You are kind to me, kinder even than at first. You didn't run after the younger men, rich or poor." Then he said with awe in his voice, "You have come to me. Do not be afraid. I'll do just as you ask. Everyone knows you are a woman of the most beautiful heart and soul."

"But Ruth," he said, forcing himself to speak the truth, not wanting anything to come between them now, "though it's true that I am your kinsman, there is another man who is more closely related than I. By law, he should marry you instead."

He heard the frightened breath she took, the way she felt for his hand in the darkness and held it hard. Joy and fear nearly broke his heart. He would give half his land to Japheth if need be to purchase this precious jewel. Ruth must be his. He pressed her hand gently and motioned to a place on the threshing floor.

"Stay here for the night, and in the morning if this man wants to do his duty as your guardian-redeemer, fine. I will let him redeem you. But if he is not willing, as surely as the Lord lives, I will do it."

He then covered her with his own blankets, heard her murmur agreement, and felt more than anything the way she clung to his hand an instant longer than was necessary. That God should give him this gift was beyond the dream of his heart. When she lay quiet, he too laid down, his face to the stars. Loneliness no longer yawned beneath him. Ruth, the fairest, most righteous of women, would be his own. *Blessed be God!*

And now, all women, call me blessed. Wife of Boaz, daughter of Naomi, mother of the brightest-eyed son that ever came to this earth, I am rich beyond all my dreams. My journey to this place has been long. I have toiled, and I have waited. I have trusted when the God I claimed led me by paths where I could see no hope. But all of it has brought me here, to this joyous good, this gift of a life beyond my imagining.

When I returned to Naomi that morning, after my visit to Boaz, she took one look at my face and knew his answer. I was panicked at the thought of this relative, this strange man who could ruin the hope of my heart. But I should have known the kindness of God better than that. Naomi heard my fear and flicked it away with wave of her hand.

"Boaz, my dear Ruth, will not rest until he has seen the end of it,"

she said, my face in her hands.

And he didn't. I suspect, though he staunchly denies it, that he dealt with Japheth behind all our backs. I care only that the ending of the tale was that Boaz was mine, and I his. When Japheth declared, before the village, that he claimed no right to me, Boaz shouted in joy. The elders grinned, and the old men cackled. And when I stepped out the door, a flock of women kissed my face and hands and crowed with joy.

And now I stand in the doorway of my home, eyes on the fields of my husband. Boaz's straight form is striding home to me in the starlit dusk. The moon is full in the sky tonight, a bright face like that of the God I love. When my journey with him began, his light was beyond me, a good I reached out to when I was afraid. Then it was a star I followed, blind but trusting, into a new land. Now the light of God is the beat of my heart, the song of my life. Through every change, the brightness of my God remains. And finally, I am home.

devotional

I was halfway through the writing of this book when I decided to take a break and head out on a road trip. I had a book tour coming up and friends to visit, but my heart was as restless as the autumn wind shaking the aspens outside my window. I was restless with desire, desperate for answers to prayers I had prayed for many years, desperate for a miracle.

For years I had followed God, and I was thirsting for some reward. I couldn't sit another minute at home with no hope of husband, friend, or future. So I planned my trip and offered a presumptious challenge to God: He had three weeks to zap me with a life plan. I craved answers of the etched-in-stone sort. With that, I bundled into my little blue hatchback and drove down the dawn.

First came quiet. I had countless stacks of music and audiobooks to distract me for days of driving, but in the hush of my car, away from the phone and computer, I became still enough to pray. I wrangled and begged, talking aloud over the hum of my engine, demanding that God take away my confusion. To send me a little hope.

Then came people. A nonstop round of souls, each with a story of joy but also pain. I met new friends and caught up with old ones. I heard of times both hard and blessed, of lives marked by cancer or romance. Good and ill, hope and pain, all intertwined in a life story. But it was the pain I noticed most, the yearning and unanswered prayers that stabbed the hearts of my friends and new acquaintances.

Our late-night talks centered mostly on what we hoped for, things we prayed God would remember before we gave up waiting. I found that others shared my dilemma in direction, my loneliness, my want for God to give or lead.

We all want and wait for something. Many of our prayers go unanswered. A question now filled up the silence of my days on the road: How can I be sure of God?

Then, one evening, a friend asked me a question that dug down to the depths of my heart and shook me wide awake: *What would it be like to face the world entirely without God?* His question echoed in my mind all the next day as I drove through the rollicking hills of Virginia, the trees around me afire with fall colors. A thousand other questions came on its heels.

What if I bore these needs and could not speak them in prayer or beg for grace? What if there was no love to bear my whimpers and whines? What if I truly gave up my trust in God? I saw then what blackness could be, what real confusion would feel like, and how despair would taste. I had spent my whole trip in a desperate plea for answers to all of my questions. I wanted to be sure of my life, my money, my friends, and my plans. But that morning, God showed me that the only thing I needed to be absolutely sure of was *Him*.

When I set out on this journey of loving God and following Him all my days, He didn't promise me an easy life or a mansion or a sure-fire ten-year investment plan. The God who created the universe promised to personally sustain me. He guaranteed me that a love greater than any human affection would cradle me throughout my days.

Could I trust God with all of my life? Would I live out the decision I made when I first chose to give my heart to God? Would I now give Him *all* of myself—my dear little dreams and girlish hopes as well as the momentous decisions?

Ruth trusted in that way. Ruth gave the deepest desires of her heart to God and left them in His hands. Her journey began with the loss of everything she had known. She had no money or plan. She had nothing to fall back on when she arrived in Bethlehem. There was no guarantee of help or food, no promised friend, and no prospective husbands. For all she knew, she would die a poor, old maid in a foreign land.

But Ruth didn't live by fear. She chose to trust in God with all her heart no matter how bleak the road ahead looked. The wonderful thing about Ruth's story is that in her life we see the outcome of faith. If ever anyone found the quintessential happy ending of prince, palace, and progeny, it was Ruth. From outcast widow to beloved wife, this is the sort of reward we all yearn for.

I chose to end this book with the story of Ruth because in it we see the sweet, miraculous grace of a woman who trusted God and saw His incredible reward. And it is this hope for a happy ending that keeps us walking, keeps us trusting. Yes, I'm still battling spiders and trying to figure out my finances. I'm still in the place where much faithfulness and grit are needed for me to keep going and trust God with the desires of my heart. But the story of Ruth convinces me that God knows exactly what I need that He will fill the desires of my heart in His time.

God is the bringer of hope. He is the maker of happy endings.

What do I hope for? I hope for my Boaz (or Darcy, as he is more commonly known among my friends). I yearn for friendship. Not the casual, chatty kind we experience in the five minutes before church starts, but the deep kind—the sort of companionship that is a shelter and a feast shared by two kindred souls. I long for the sure knowledge that I am doing the work for which I was made and growing the kingdom along with it. And as a confirmed nomad who has moved at least twenty times, I long for the security and rootedness of a long-term home.

What about you? What do you wait for? What do you hope for? When you lay down at night, what fills your thoughts and shapes your dreams? Can you trust them to God and wait for His happy ending?

If there is one thing I have gotten into my thick, worried, struggling head this year, it's the realization that God has always been there, loving and leading me even as I screamed at His absence. Even my road trip, my desperate attempt at distraction, turned out to be His grace. Not only did I come to realize that God alone was certain, I was met with friendship, strengthened by extended times of prayer, and heartened by freedom of the open road. God opened my eyes to see that He had been working in my heart minute by minute even when I thought He had forgotten me.

That is the truth Ruth understood, and it is the truth we must embrace if we are going to survive and thrive in this thing called life. We must believe heart and soul that God knows our desires, our hopes, and secret dreams. We must trust that He is wise beyond our thoughts and the road He leads us on is truly good, no matter how hard or long it seems.

If you choose to follow God, if you make the daring choice to be one of those women who asks the Almighty to invade your days, you're in for the adventure of a lifetime. Loving God doesn't mean a Disney life where you get a prince and castle because you followed enough rules. God is the great and beautiful lover of our hearts, and we are the sinful and broken people He loves. Life with God means His Holy Spirit will doggedly root sin out of your heart and form faith in your soul. It means you will be called to fight against the darkness and navigate a journey down a narrow, holy road. Loving God doesn't mean having a perfect or easy life. It means trusting in a perfect God who is ready to make us just what we need to be.

And what about the great reward? A Ruth-sort of happy ending? Yes, I believe that God will bring us even that. God knows us better than anyone else. Our hopes are cradled in his hands. I haven't come to the end (or even the middle) of my tale yet. I carry a pack full of hopes. I walk accompanied by dreams. But God will send them in His time, and like Ruth, I will rejoice when He does.

Boaz and hope and home, here I come!

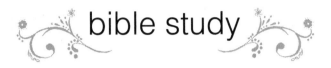

bible study

Psalm 139

Read this psalm all the way through and insert your own name wherever you can. Do you think God is intimately "familiar" with all your ways? What is your greatest secret desire? Do you trust Him to hold this for you?

2 Chronicles 15:1–9

The stories of the Old Testament kings often centered on whether or not they trusted God. When God told Asa to "be strong," what did He also promise? What reward do you hope to receive from God?

Psalm 27:13–14

When does David (who composed this psalm) believe he will see God's goodness? Do you believe that God will reward you, not just in heaven, but here on earth too? How can hope for reward keep us from despair?

Psalm 33:16–22

Who has God's eye? What are we to do when we are in trouble? Will God keep us as we wait for our deepest dreams to come true?

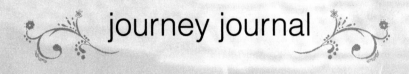

journey journal